Property of M. Rodgers

PRINCE2® in Practice

Other publications by Van Haren Publishing

Van Haren Publishing (VHP) specializes in titles on Best Practices, methods and standards within four domains:
- IT management,
- Architecture (Enterprise and IT),
- Business management and
- Project management

These publications are grouped in series: *ITSM Library, Best Practice and IT Management Topics*. VHP is also publisher on behalf of leading companies and institutions: The Open Group, IPMA-NL, PMI-NL, CA, Getronics, Pink Elephant.

Topics are (per domain):

IT (Service) Management / IT Governance	Architecture (Enterprise and IT)	Project/Programme/ Risk Management
ASL	Archimate®	A4 Project management
BiSL	GEA®	ICB / NCB
CATS	TOGAF™	MINCE®
CMMI		M_o_R®
CobiT	**Business Management**	MSP
ISO 17799	EFQM	PMBoK®
ISO 27001	ISA-95	PRINCE2®
ISO/IEC 20000	ISO 9000	
ISPL	ISO 9001:2000	
IT Service CMM	SixSigma	
ITIL® V2	SOX	
ITIL® V3	SqEME®	
ITSM		
MOF		
MSF		

For the latest information on VHP publications, visit our website: www.vanharen.net.

PRINCE2® in Practice

A practical approach to creating project management documents

How to avoid bulky, inaccessible, stand alone, and illegible documents

Henny Portman

Title:	PRINCE2® in Practice - A practical approach to creating project management documents
Author:	Henny Portman
Editor:	Steve Newton
Publisher:	Van Haren Publishing, Zaltbommel, www.vanharen.net
ISBN:	978 90 8753 328 1
Print:	First edition, first impression, April 2009
Layout and design:	CO2 Premedia, Amersfoort - NL
Copyright:	Original edition in Dutch: *De Praktische PRINCE® - Maakt het weer leuk*, 2de druk, © 2009, Uitgeverij Dialoog, Amersfoort – NL This English translation: © 2009, Van Haren Publishing, Zaltbommel - NL

© Crown copyright material taken from the Office of Government Commerce publication, Managing Successful Projects with PRINCE2, is reproduced with the permission of the Controller of HMSO and Queen's Printer for Scotland.

For any further enquiries about Van Haren Publishing, please send an e-mail to: info@vanharen.net. Although this publication has been composed with most care, neither Author nor Editor nor Publisher can accept any liability for damage caused by possible errors and/or incompleteness in this publication.

No part of this publication may be reproduced in any form by print, photo print, microfilm or any other means without written permission by the Publisher.

Preface

I have been head of the Project Management Office of a financial institution for some time. I am responsible for the organisation and professionalization of projects and programmes. I also take care of the guidance, coaching and training of project managers.

The management of the institution for which I work has chosen PRINCE2® as the standard for project management. We have set up and implemented a comprehensive training course for project managers. In addition to behaviour training, PRINCE2 foundation and practitioner training have also been included.

A great deal of literature is available on PRINCE2. Judging by the number of publications, a new book about PRINCE2 seems redundant. However, this is not the case. The existing books mainly describe the theory behind PRINCE2. The stages, relevant processes and underlying sub-processes are discussed, usually accompanied by the relevant techniques. What I missed in my organisation with the introduction of PRINCE2, was a pragmatic approach to translate formal reports into practice: how could we make PRINCE2 practical? There were indeed reporting criteria, but these criteria were useful enough. Executives either did not read the documents or could not recognize the main ideas. I therefore needed a pragmatic translation trick. Because such a trick did not exist, I created it myself. The approach that I describe in this book has subsequently been successfully applied by my organisation.

The points of departure of our approach generate the familiar management products, such as the Project Brief, the Project Initiation Document, and the Project Board Report. I have stripped these products of technical jargon under the catchwords 'KISS' (Keep It Short and Simple) and 'business in the driver seat'. Project managers and executives can use them together.

This book is meant for everyone who has anything to do with project management. It is for:
- the line manager who wants to bring about change and base a temporary organisation on it;
- the head of the Project Management Office who is looking for handles to create a professionalizing device; and
- the project manager who has adopted the PRINCE2 theory and now wants to apply this theory in practice.

But the book is also meant for experienced project managers who wish to improve their relationship with their executive, and project managers who want to manage instead of getting bogged down in the filling in of endless documents and templates. This book is to be used particularly as a reference book.

In 2009 the PRINCE2 version 2009 is introduced. In respect of the first Dutch release of this book, I have adapted the terminology and classification of the PRINCE2 products, based on the information that was available at the beginning of 2009. The most important changes between PRINCE2 version 2005 and PRINCE2 version 2009 are indicated in the table over the page.

	2005	2009
Principles	-	7 Principles
Themes	8 Components	7 Main Themes (Configuration Management has lapsed)
Processes	8 Processes	7 Processes (Drawing up a plan has lapsed)
Sub-processes	45 Sub-processes	-
Techniques	3 Techniques	References to other OGC methods and techniques
Project Management Documents	36 Documents	27 Documents
Project Environment	-	Description recorded

Table 0.1   Summary of differences between PRINCE2 versions 2005 and 2009

This English translation takes account of these differences. The chapters relating to the documentation framework and the PRINCE2 documents and building blocks have not been radically changed. PRINCE2 principles and project environment are added to chapter 1 as additional aspects. The PRINCE2 components in Chapter 4 are replaced by the PRINCE2 themes (with the reference Th1 to Th7 inclusive). Additionally I have included the PRINCE2 techniques, 'Product-based Planning' and 'Quality Control' despite the fact that these techniques are not described in PRINCE2 version 2009.

I owe many thanks to colleagues who provided comments on the draft versions. I would like to mention Ben van Berkel, project manager at Van Aetsveld, Erik-Jan Dokter, project controller at Inland Revenue, Eric Plooij, senior project manager at Atos Consulting, Richard Wijkstra, senior project manager at Getronics PinkRoccade and finally, Chris Boogert, project manager at Van Aetsveld. Chris tested the approach in practice.

To support implementation, the templates and spreadsheets are available via the product page for this book on the vanharen.net web shop.

Without a doubt this book is still not taking account of all aspects of a PRINCE2 implementation. The readers should not lose sight of their environment when implementing the PRINCE2 documents. They can simply adapt the templates on offer. I am naturally prepared to help achieve this translation through the use of workshops. I sincerely welcome any reactions and feedback and look forward to hearing from you.

Houten - NL, 2009
Henny Portman

Henny.portman@planet.nl

Contents

    Preface V

1 Different ways of looking at PRINCE2 1
    1.1   The PRINCE2 Process Model 3
    1.2   PRINCE2 themes 4
    1.3   The PRINCE2 principles 5
    1.4   The PRINCE2 documents 6
    1.5   The project environment 8
    1.6   The role of the project manager 9

2 Documentation and reporting standard, the framework 11
    2.1   PRINCE2 made practical 11
    2.2   Storyboarding: reporting with presentations 12
    2.3   Building block concept 13
    2.4   Use 16

3 The PRINCE2 documents 19
    3.1   Mandate (D1) 20
    3.2   Business Case (D2) 21
    3.3   Project Brief (D3) 23
    3.4   Project Initiation Document (PID) 25
    3.5   Work Package (D5) 27
    3.6   The Status Report (D6) 28
    3.7   End Project Report (D7) 30
    3.8   Exceptions Report (D8) 31
    3.9   Lessons Report (D9) 32
    3.10   Issue Register (D10) 33
    3.11   Risk Register (D11) 34
    3.12   Lessons Learned Register (D12) 35
    3.13   Summary 36

4 Relationship with the PRINCE2 themes 37
    4.1   Business Case (Th1) 37
    4.2   Organisation (Th2) 38
    4.3   Planning (Th3) 41
    4.4   Progress Assessment (Th4) 41
    4.5   Risk Management (Th5) 44
    4.6   Quality in projects (Th6) 45
    4.7   Change Management (Th7) 47
    4.8   Summary 47

5 Relationship with the techniques 49
    5.1   Product-Based Planning (T1) 49
    5.2   Quality Check (T2) 50
    5.3   Configuration Management (T3) 51
    5.4   Lessons Learned and Customer Satisfaction (T4) 53
    5.5   Summary 54

6 Developments and trends 55
    6.1   Project and portfolio management systems 55
    6.2   Integration of PPM tools and the document approach 56
    6.3   'SMART' templates and building blocks 57
    6.4   Summary 58

7 From theory to practice 59
    7.2   A real-life example 61

8 The documentation building blocks 65
    8.1   Document Management (B1) 67
    8.2   Mandate - <number> <project name> (B2) 69
    8.3   Project background - <project name> (B3) 70
    8.4   Scope - <project name> (B4) 71
    8.5   Business Case risk analysis - <project name> (B5) 72
    8.6   Cost benefit cash flow - <project name> (B6) 73
    8.7   Project approach - <project name> (B7) 75
    8.8   Value Chain - <project name> (B8) 77
    8.9   Product Breakdown 78
    8.10   Product breakdown - <project name> Work package - <work package name> (B10) . . 80
    8.11   Product description - <project name> <name> (B11) 81
    8.12   Resources - <project name> (B12) 82
    8.13   Planning <date> - <project name> (B13) 83
    8.14   Risks - <project name> (B14) 84
    8.15   Organisation (B15) 86
    8.16   Budget details <date> - <project name> (B16) 88
    8.17   Acceptance criteria - <project name> (B17) 90
    8.18   Architectural and security aspects <project name> (B18) 91
    8.19   Business process aspects - <project name> (B19) 93
    8.20   Communication plan - <project name> (B20) 94
    8.21   Quality plan - <project name> (B21) 95
    8.22   Highlights Report <date> - <project name> (B22) 96
    8.23   Decisions to be taken <date> - <project name> (B23) 98
    8.24   Recapitulation - <Project name> (B24) 99
    8.25   Follow-on Action Recommendations - <project name> (B25) 100
    8.26   Lessons Report - <project name> (B26) 101
    8.27   Project Board Actions/Decisions (B27) 102
    8.28   Customer Satisfaction (B28) 103
    8.29   Project Team Satisfaction (B29) 104
    8.30   Issue Register (B30) 105
    8.31   Risk Register (B31) 106
    8.32   Lessons Learned Register (B32) 107
    8.33   Action list (B33) 108

Appendix A: Dutch - English translation list 109
Bibliography 117
About the author 119
Index 121

1 Different ways of looking at PRINCE2

'Cheshire Puss,' Alice said timidly, 'Would you tell me please, which way I ought to go from here?' 'That depends a good deal on where you want to get to,' said the Cat. 'I don't much care,' said Alice. 'Then it doesn't matter much which way you go,' said the cat. 'so long as I get somewhere,' Alice added as an explanation.
'Oh, you're sure to do that,' said the Cat, 'if you only walk long enough.'
(From Alice in Wonderland by Lewis Carroll)

PRINCE2 books offer enough handles to enable you to get a grip on the management processes. However, the behavioural aspects are not really addressed in these books. For the soft side of project management there are other books. I would like to mention two in particular: first of all, 'The Little Prince' by Antoine de Saint-Exupéry (2002). This is a lovely little book from which to read aloud. The book is also very suitable for the project manager. It teaches the project manager to view their world in a different way. You can obtain the following lessons from this book:

- to observe without bias;
- to identify confusing problems;
- not to define problems too quickly;
- not to formulate any solutions;
- to defer your own opinions and judgements;
- to allow other points of view;
- to leave room for interpretations;
- to think in terms of events.

The second one is 'De Kleine Prinses' by the Dutch authors Nicoline Mulder and Fokke Wijnstra (2008). They dwell on the softer aspects of projects, such as value passion, the objective behind the result and the meaning of the result for the organisation.

'The Chaos Report' of the Standish Group (see www.standishgroup.com) and the survey report 'Benchmark ICT Projectmanagement Nederland 2006, Progressie in professie?' ('Benchmark ICT Project Management Netherlands 2006, Progression in Profession?') show that in the Netherlands almost half of projects overrun their time and one third of projects exceed the agreed budget. The scope definition is seen by researchers as the greatest risk. The recent survey, 'Benchmark ICT Projectmanagement Nederland 2007, Transformatie met Project Portfolio Management' ('Benchmark ICT Project Management Netherlands 2007, Transformation with Project Portfolio Management') shows an even greater deterioration in respect of 2006: half the projects have a longer completion time and only 58% of the projects are delivered on budget. In my opinion project managers and executives do not learn enough from mistakes made. Lessons learned are not recorded. Coordination between products and the scope of the project is not clear enough. In part this can be traced back to poor application of project management. In the investigation 'Benchmark Projectmanagement 2008, Transparantie tussen Project en Organisatie' (Benchmark Project Management 2008, Transparency between Project and Organisation), one of the conclusions is that 'Organisations are slow to learn in respect of project management'.

"There is nothing more difficult to handle, more doubtful of success and more dangerous to carry through than introducing a new system in an organisation. The innovator makes enemies of all those who prospered under the old system and only lukewarm support is forthcoming from those who would prosper under the new.'
(From The Prince by Niccolò Machiavelli)

This book lets you view PRINCE2 through another pair of eyes. Naturally, processes are important, but in this book I follow the PRINCE2 documents in particular. You are given a pragmatic tool through which you can put the flesh onto the introduction of PRINCE2. With this, project managers and Project Board members are able to manage their projects effectively and efficiently.

Traditional PRINCE2 books use three perspectives (spectacles) to deal with PRINCE2. These are the PRINCE2 process model, the PRINCE2 components and the PRINCE2 principles. This book adds a fourth pair of spectacles. I look at PRINCE2 in terms of the project management documents. I follow the PRINCE2 process in terms of the products: Mandate, Project Brief, Project Initiation Document, Exceptions Report, Status Report (Project Board Report) and End Project Report. I show how these documents in PRINCE2 are built up step-by-step, how it is possible to re-implement building blocks and how consistency of information in the documents is guaranteed. I follow the course from the Project Brief to the Project Initiation Document and show how the Project Brief forms the basis of the Project Initiation Document.

In conclusion, PRINCE2 can be represented as follows:

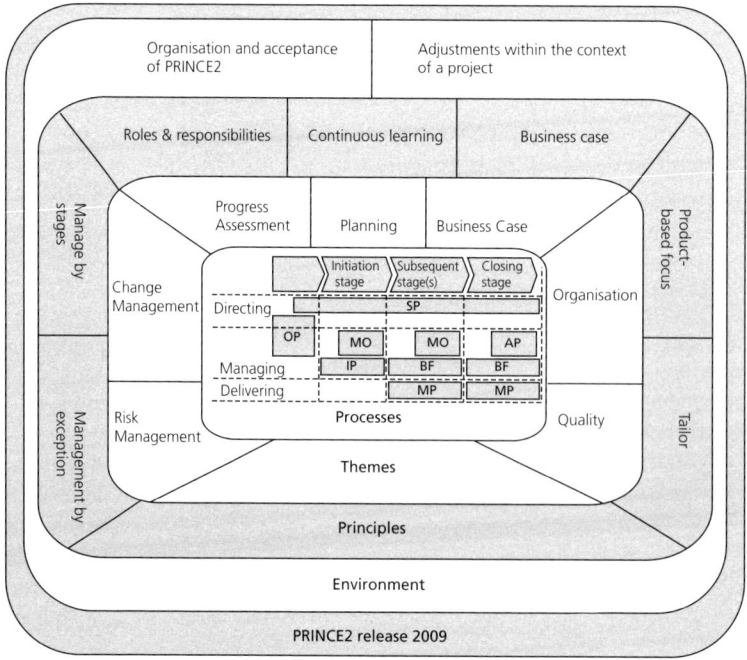

Figure 1.1   PRINCE2 version 2009

The following sections briefly describe what the spectacles show you.

1.1 The PRINCE2 Process Model

The first pair of spectacles shows that in PRINCE2 the project management process is subdivided into Pre-project Stage, Initiation Stage, Continuation Stage(s) and the Closing Stage. Within these stages the model distinguishes between seven main processes (as seen from the point of view of the Project Board and the Project Manager).

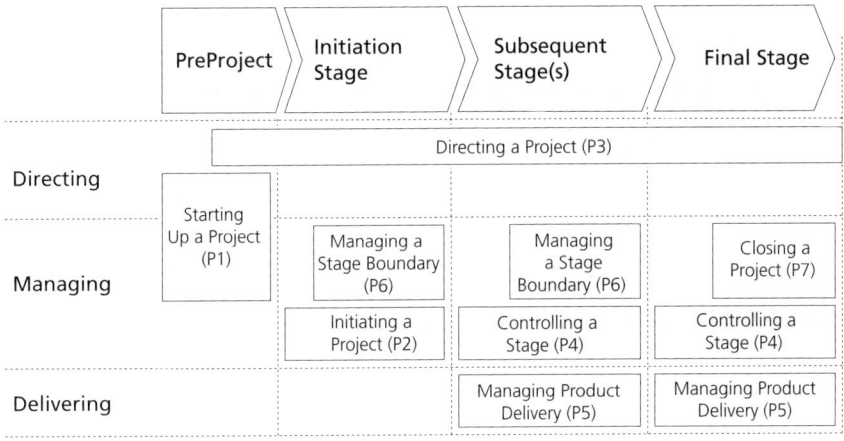

Figure 1.2 The PRINCE2 Process Model (Source: OGC)

Within the PRINCE2 Process Model we identify the sections Directing, Managing and Delivering. The Directing and the Managing levels use the process 'Starting up a Project'. A PRINCE2 project consists of at least two management stages, the first of which is always the Initiation Stage. The process 'Managing Stage Boundaries' appears for the first time at the end of the Initiation Stage and is repeated at the end of all following stages, with the exception of the End Stage. This later stage has the process 'Closing a Project'.

The seven main processes are:

- *P1: Starting up a Project (SP)* This is the first process in PRINCE2, and precedes the start of the project. It ensures that all information is made available to initiate the project. The process provides an interim Business Case. This provides answers to questions about the reason for the project, the advantages, the risks, the costs and the benefits. Sometimes alternatives are worked out.

- *P2: Initiating a Project (IP)* This is the first process in a project. This process ensures that all parties concerned are aware of the products or services that the project is going to deliver, the times at which this will be happening, the costs and the quality requirements. In addition, the process explains which staff members are needed to achieve the objectives. Finally the management and the responsibilities associated with the project are made clear.

- *P3: Directing a Project (DP)* This process occurs within the Project Board of the project. It runs from 'Starting up a Project' up to and including 'Closing a Project'. The objective of the process is the successful execution and delivery of the results of the project.

- *P4: Controlling a Stage (CS)* This process describes the daily activities of the project manager during the execution of the project.

- *P5: Managing Product Delivery (MP)* This process specifies the management activities for delivery of the product. In the case of outsourcing it may be possible that third parties could be responsible. The project manager would then come to agreements with this third party about costs, delivery time and quality requirements. Whoever is responsible for the tasks performs them independently of the project manager.

- *P6: Managing Stage Boundaries (SB)* This process describes the activities undertaken by the project manager to close a stage and the activities to start the preparation for the next stage.

- *P7: Closing a Project (CP)* This process states the activities required to close the project and to release the project manager from his commitments.

1.2   PRINCE2 themes

In addition to processes, PRINCE2 has themes. The project manager uses these themes in the execution of the processes, and organises and directs the project.

- *Th1: Business Case (why)* The Business Case of the project is a description of the end result in terms of costs and benefits. Every project must contribute to the objectives of the organisation.

- *Th2: Organisation (who)* The setting up of the project organisation (Project Board, project group, work groups) where the tasks, qualifications and responsibilities are also described. The project manager further negotiates agreements with the project staff members in relation to their tasks. He ensures that these staff members receive the time and authority to execute their tasks.

- *Th3: Planning (where, how, when and how much)* PRINCE2 has an overall project plan for the project and a detailed stage plan for every stage. For (part) products the delivery times must be clear.

- *Th4: Progress Assessment* This makes it possible to take decisions at the correct moments. Reporting on the progress of, and the exceptions within, the project diminishes the chance of exceeding agreed timescales and budget.

- *Th5: Risk Management (what if)* The identification, assessment and control of uncertainty or risks and appropriate countermeasures.

- *Th6: Quality* All products must comply with quality requirements that are fixed beforehand. At the beginning of the project it is determined who is going to execute the necessary checks.

- *Th7: Change Management* Change Management takes care of the assessment and controlled implementation of changes in the products. How changes are dealt with during a project is a determining factor for success. Through the use of change management it is possible to execute changes in a monitored and controlled manner. PRINCE2 differentiates between changes in the specification of a product (RfC: Request for Change) and changes resulting from indicated errors (Off specification).

1.3 The PRINCE2 principles

PRINCE2 principles are universal, self-explanatory and enable the project manager to achieve results.

- *Pr1: Business Case* In a PRINCE2 project, testing with reference to the Business Case happens continually.

- *Pr2: Continuous learning* PRINCE2 project teams learn from previous experiences (lessons learnt are identified and recorded during execution).

- *Pr3: Roles and responsibilities* PRINCE2 projects have predetermined and agreed roles and responsibilities within the project organisation, so that the executive, users and suppliers can feel that they are given recognition.

- *Pr4: Manage by stages* A PRINCE2 project is planned, assessed and managed on a stage-by-stage basis.

- *Pr5: Management by Exception* A PRINCE2 project is characterized by particular tolerances for all project objectives (time as well as budget and quality of the to be delivered products).

- *Pr6: Product-based focus* A PRINCE2 project focuses on the definition and delivery of products. The scope and quality criteria are of particular importance.

- *Pr7: Tailor* PRINCE2 can take account of variances in relation to the size, environment, complexity and importance of a project, the competences of the participants and the associated risks of a project.

1.4 The PRINCE2 documents

The last pair of spectacles views the project management documents and the corresponding work sequence. That is the basis of this book. These spectacles give an abstract account of PRINCE2. They allow you to see that during the process steps the basis is created for the subsequent processes. During the follow-on steps the project manager can supplement the documents with new information in the form of building blocks. I follow the PRINCE2 process in terms of the documents: Mandate, Project Brief, Project Initiation Document, Exceptions Report, Status Report (Project Board Reporting) and End Project Report.

The documents are the result of, and the input to, PRINCE2 processes. The Mandate is, for example, the input to the process 'Starting up a project'. The executive receives the documents. This emphasises that he is in charge. Expansion or simplification of project management products as a consequence of the size of the project is very possible.

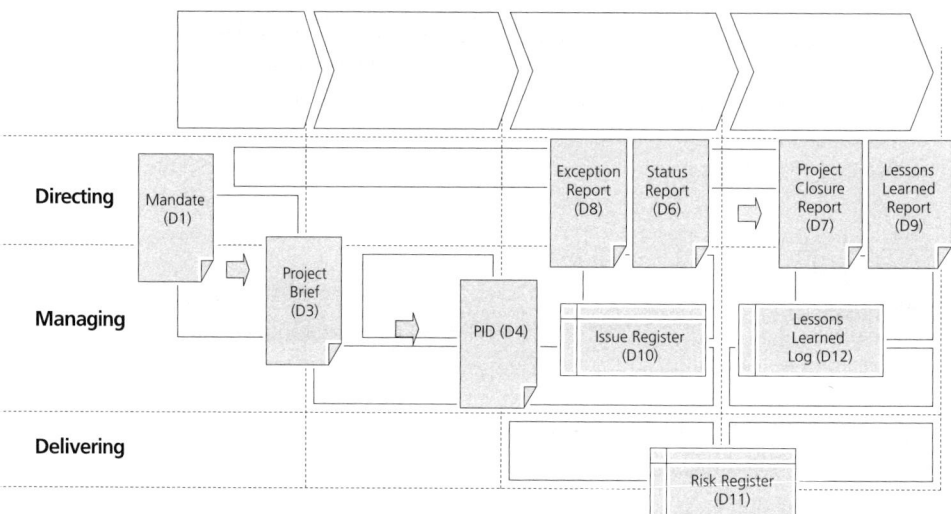

Figure 1.3   PRINCE2 documents (Based on source: OGC)

The most important project management documents are:

- *D1: Mandate* This is the commencing point for starting up the project. The mandate gives a short description of the reasons for the project, the objectives of the project and the products to be delivered.

- *D2: Business Case*[1] This document describes the reasons for the start and the continuation of the project. It presents the expected costs and benefits. During the project this document is tested and re-adjusted if necessary.

---

[1] The document D2 Business Case is not included in Figure 1.3. It is a part of the D3 Project Brief.

- *D3: Project Brief* This is a description of the proposed project in terms of the Business Case, initial risks, potential resources or needed roles and high level approach. After approval, the project brief constitutes the point of departure for initiating the project.

- *D4: Project Initiation Document (PID)* This document describes all relevant information for the stakeholders of the project (including the project manager). In this document the products, the planned delivery times and the necessary materials, tools and people are described. The PID further provides insight into the required budget and quality requirements. The PID is the norm that assesses the progress of the project and, in the event of changes, that decides on the continuation of the project.

- *D5: Work Package* The work package provides all the information that is necessary to develop the products. It includes the composition of the work package and the accompanying product descriptions.[2]

- *D6: Status Report (or Project Board Report)* The Status Report is the document intended for the Project Board. It reveals how the project is progressing in relation to the plan and the budget.

- *D7: Project End Report (closure document)* This document is the concluding product of the project. This contains the account of the products delivered. In addition the document compares the original plan, budget and quality requirements as they are stated in the PID. A current business case is part of the project end report. It also includes recommendations on how to deal with any outstanding issues.

- *D8: Exceptions Report* The Exceptions Report describes any exceptions encountered during the project. Through reference to analyses (including the effect on budget, planning and quality) it shows alternative ways to address new situations.

- *D9: Lessons Report* This document states the lessons learned from the project. What went well and what was less successful? Which lessons have been learned? After the Project Board has approved this document, it is made available for future projects.

- *D10: Issue Register* This is a list with all the issues encountered in the project (problems, new requirements, lapsed requirements). Every issue contains an explanation, manner of assessment, establishment of priorities, decisions taken and current status.

- *D11: Risk Register* This is a continuously expanding document that consists of a summary of the risks, the impact, probability, the proposed countermeasures or actions to be taken to reduce the risk and the responsibility of managing the risk reduction.

- *D12: Lessons Learned Register* This is also a continuously expanding document containing an overview of the lessons learned during the project.

---

[2] The document Work Package is not included in Figure 1.3. It is included as part of the D4 Project Initiation Document.

In addition to the spectacles described briefly above, PRINCE2 looks at the role of the project manager and at the environment in which the project is executed. The following sections examine this more closely.

1.5 The project environment

PRINCE2 provides recommendations for use within an organisation. In addition, PRINCE2 also contains suggestions for the adaptation of a project so that each project can be precisely customized.

With the organisation and acceptance of PRINCE2, attention is directed to the following aspects in particular:

- ownership of the project management process;
- rules and guidelines for the scalability of PRINCE2;
- standards (documentation templates, definitions);
- training and development strategy;
- integration with business processes;
- tools;
- guarantees.

The project team itself adapts PRINCE2 to the specific circumstances of the project. In this the project team can be guided by:

- the size of the project;
- the independence of the project (or is it a subdivision of a programme?);
- the type of project (product development, policy, construction…);
- use of specific methods or frameworks in the project.

In addition the team will come to agreements about:

- roles to be allocated and responsibilities;
- project management products to be used;
- number, scope and nature of the stages;
- reporting and assessment;
- tolerances;
- use of PRINCE2 processes.

1.6 The role of the project manager

In addition to competence in the application of the method, PRINCE2 requires the following skills in a project manager:

- leadership skills;
- to be open to conviction;
- to be able to deal with conflict;
- negotiation skills;
- ability to motivate;
- ability to solve problems.

PRINCE2 describes how the project manager can cooperate with the Project Board and the project team and which management responsibilities are required.

Many books have been published on the ideas behind PRINCE2. In the introductory chapter I have shown that we can look at PRINCE2 through four pairs of spectacles. I have also briefly mentioned a number of PRINCE2 concepts such as the project environment and the role of the project manager. The existing books describe PRINCE2 processes, themes and principles in particular. In this chapter I have added a fourth pair of spectacles, namely the PRINCE2 Project Management Documents. These spectacles show that during the PRINCE2 process steps, documents are generated that become the basis of the processes that follow. During these follow-on processes the documents are completed. In the rest of this book we follow the PRINCE2 processes by means of the Products Mandate, Project Brief, Project Initiation Document, Exceptions Report, Status Report (Project Board Report) and End Project Report. The next chapter considers the sequence of the documents. In addition I also look at duplication in the documents and at efficiency in the production of documents.

2 Documentation and reporting standard, the framework

'Decide on what you think is right, and stick to it'
George Eliot (1819-1880), English novelist

In the previous chapter we have seen that you can look at PRINCE2 through document spectacles. In this chapter we examine the documents more closely. I look at the relationship (sequence) between the documents and their construction. We are all familiar with project plans and project initiation documents (PIDs) of fifty pages or more. Are there any Project Board members that ever read these? How many Project Board members have searched through these documents for the project scope and for their tasks and responsibilities in the project?

2.1 PRINCE2 made practical

Some organisations that have chosen the PRINCE2 project management methodology use the templates in an inflexible manner. The PRINCE2 manual, however, does not have any templates. You are expected to develop these yourself. The manual describes the information that is to be processed in the documents. PRINCE2 argues that an organisation should apply the required translation trick themselves.

A Google search produced more than 10,000 hits in respect of PRINCE2 templates, including the official PRINCE2 site of OGC. Templates keep the project management professionals busy. In my experience project management documents that are based on templates often have the following characteristics:

- they are standalone;
- they are descriptive and not concise;
- they leave room for interpretation;
- they are labour-intensive to complete;
- they are bothersome to read;
- they are aimed at formal accountability/reporting.

This begs the following question:

Is it possible to provide stakeholders with adequate information without falling into the trap of bulky, inaccessible, standalone, and illegible documents?

If the answer to this question is positive, then it should also be possible to enhance the quality of projects. After all, the stakeholders gain a better insight, which brings about more effective and efficient decision making by the Project Board. The project manager can be more focused upon managing the project instead of writing bulky (progress) reports. In the search for an answer to this question I used *storyboarding* and the concept of building blocks.

2.2 Storyboarding: reporting with presentations

Storyboarding is a technique where a presentation[3] is used as a report. The following characteristics apply to storyboarding:

- there is a logical sequence of the pictures;
- there is coherence between pictures;
- the structure can be compared to a traditional report (list of contents, chapters and paragraphs);
- a good storyboard makes a descriptive report redundant;
- it aims for optimal legibility, reflecting only what is essential;
- it is directed at decisions.

Every picture is standalone and consists of a headline with a message (horizontal logic). Ideally the headlines are linked content-wise. The picture supports the message (vertical logic). In principle there are no sequential pictures on the same topic. Every picture contains only one message. If you read only the headlines (horizontally), you get the gist of the story.

In addition to being used as a technique to present reports, the concept of storyboarding is also used in the film industry. The storyboard is a collection of pictures outlining situations from a film script as envisaged by the director. Sometimes storyboards provide details, but mostly they describe the outline of the film script.

With the linking up of the picture, an uncomplicated and simple account of the story is created. Omissions and inconsistencies are immediately visible. In the rest of the book I speak of story-lines instead of storyboarding. By this I mean the series of pictures that describe the story. For examples of this, see Chapters 4 and 5 with story-lines on project resources, risks and lessons learned.

---

[3] Well-known tools (software) such as PowerPoint, OpenOffice Impress, iWork and Adobe Creative Suite can be used for this.

Figure 2.1   Example of Storyboard (film industry)

2.3   Building block concept

PRINCE2 documents consist in part of identical information blocks. Each block can be seen as a building block of a PRINCE2 document. A building block is therefore an independent subdivision of a document. Take for example the description of the background to the project. If you make a building block for this, it is information to be used in the Business Case, the Project Brief and the Project Initiation Document. The use of building blocks reduces the chance of miscommunication and the loss of information, causing de-motivation of the parties concerned.

The combination of the building blocks and the philosophy behind the storyboard (each picture is a building block) leads to the following requirements for the PRINCE2 documents:

- standardization (ensure that comparable documents for projects are built up in the same way);
- essence (no extensive passages of text, but only the necessary);
- visualization (make use of pictures, blocks, etc.: one picture says more than a thousand words).

The result of this procedure is that the executive receives the information in a recognizable and concisely represented manner. With the pressures of work, the time to read and understand documents is limited. Standardization, visualization and essence increase the possibility of reading everything, interpreting, understanding and reviewing. The executive can use his time effectively and efficiently.

Comparable arguments apply to the position of the project manager. The project manager wishes to represent the information concisely, without repeating anything and writing things up only once. The project manager has need of a handle that enforces consistency, promotes clarity and upgrades quality. The growth of a document on the basis of selected building blocks motivates and is efficient and effective.

2.3.1 Structure of PRINCE2 documents

In the development of the documentation standard I have integrated the following PRINCE2 documents (see Figure 2.2 for a simple view of the different documents and corresponding building blocks[4]):

- D1: Project Mandate;
- D2: Business Case;
- D3: Project Brief;
- D4: Project Initiation Document (PID);
- D6: Status Report;
- D7: Project End Report;
- D8: Exceptions Report.

The following sections provide an explanation of the building block philosophy. I use a simplified example for this purpose. In Chapter 3 all documents are reviewed in relation to the building blocks.

The Business Case (D2) consists of four building blocks: The Mandate, the Background of the Project, the Scope, and the Costs and Benefits Analysis (see section 3.2).

The Project Brief (D3) consists of the building blocks of the Business Case. Naturally, the content is up to date. The building blocks of the project approach and the required resources complete the Project Brief (see section 3.3).

The building blocks of the Project Brief, after being updated, form the basis of the PID (D4). The PID is created through the expansion of the Project Brief by means of the following building blocks: Project Organisation, Acceptance Criteria, Risks, Quality Plan, Architecture, Information Security, Business Processes and Product Breakdown (see section 3.4).

After the Project Board has approved the PID, the project manager will report on the progress periodically. I call this report the Status Report (D6). The basis of the Status Report consists of three building blocks from the PID: the Mandate, the Budget and the Planning. The project manager, in principle, takes the Mandate over unchanged. A change in the Mandate gives cause for the Project Board to review the Business Case once again. In addition the Budget shows how

---

[4] Not all the building blocks are shown in figure 2.2. See the fold out in the back cover of this book for the complete Overview of all the documents and building blocks.

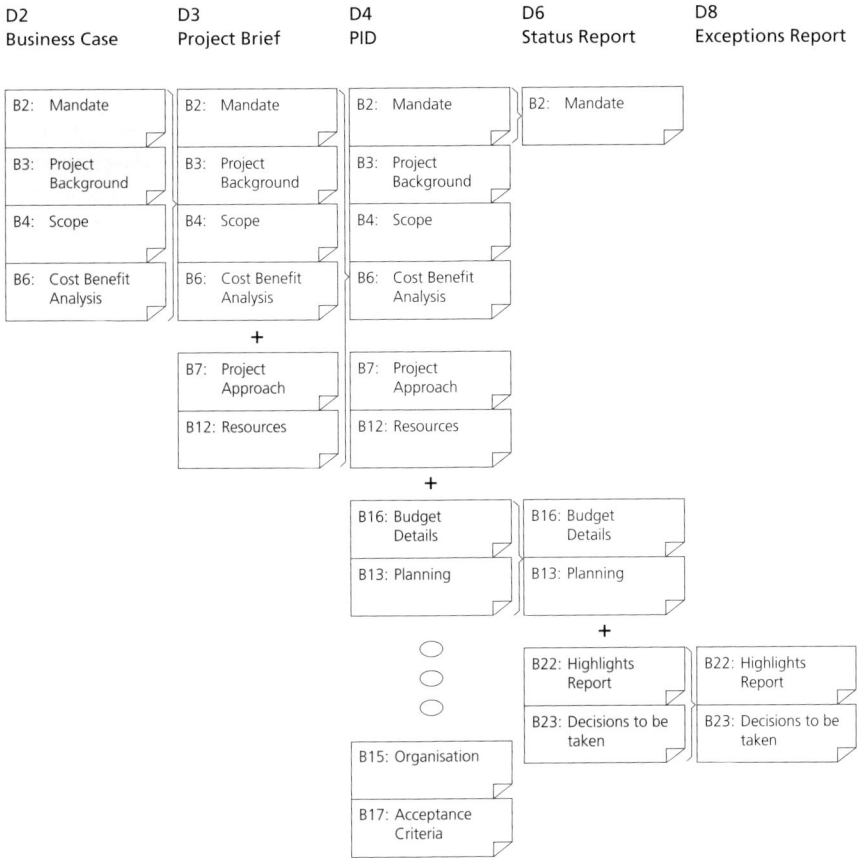

Figure 2.2 PRINCE2 document building blocks

the funds are used. The Planning indicates the progress. Both building blocks have the PID as their basis, which makes comparison with the original assumptions possible.

The fourth building block is the Highlights Report. This building block describes the most important products and includes a planning traffic light per product (item). This traffic light indicates to what extent the product is on schedule in terms of the planning. The Highlights Report likewise indicates traffic lights in respect of Project Planning, Budget, Resources, Issues and Scope. In consultation with the executive it is possible to extend the traffic lights. If there are any issues, the Highlights Report will provide information on them. In addition to the Status Report, my organisation uses a weekly Checkpoint Report. This is based on the same building blocks.

The last building block relates to the decisions that the Project Board has to make. If the project runs according to expectations, there are no decisions. In this situation it is not necessary for the Project Board to get together (the 'Management by Exception' principle of PRINCE2). Should there be a proposed decision, the consequences in terms of changes to the Budget, Planning, Scope and Resources are described (see section 3.6).

2.3.2 Templates

With graphic templates you are able to comply with the requirements of standardization, visualization and essence. The template describes the elements of a building block. This is practical for the project manager. There is little need for words. Visualization with graphics, drawings and tables is very convenient. The document can be identified by its format and use of colour. It is accessible and easy to understand. On the basis of available building blocks it enables the project manager to create quick reports and presentations.

2.3.3 Project board reporting

The project manager must also have the details easily accessible. It is for the project manager to determine how he wants the details recorded. The project manager can give his creativity free reign in the organising of the project.

2.4 Use

For some time now, the application of the proposed procedure has been utilized by a financial service provider (for projects varying from 100 000 euro to ten million euro). This organisation has developed around 25 building blocks. Each building block has its own form (template). If a building block is not relevant to a particular project, it does not make use of it at all. Project Board members endorse the omission of irrelevant building blocks. They emphasise that standardized reporting saves time. They are able to determine the status of a project quickly. The decision points provide insight.

At the time of writing this book, I gave presentations to a government authority, an energy company, a retailer, a consultancy bureau and change and project management organisations in order to bring the philosophy behind the standard into the limelight. Different organisations are currently implementing storyboards and building blocks.

It seems possible to systematically provide all concerned with adequate information without falling into the trap of bulky, inaccessible, standalone, and illegible documents. I have introduced the technique of storyboarding as a tool for reporting presentations. This promotes legibility and representation of the essence. I recommend the use of visual representations if it is possible. Storyboarding is a powerful tool to determine consistencies and omissions. I have used the overlap between PRINCE2 documents for the building block approach. Combining this with storyboarding ensures that executives and project managers use their time more effectively and efficiently.

It seems that this works:
'... A good Status Report, supported by project and executive, is an exceptionally effective and efficient means to track and manage a project...' (Remko de Jong, managing director, financial industry).

'Although formally not yet rounded off, it can be concluded in the meantime that the adoption of the practical PRINCE2 has been carried out seamlessly: The good elements have been adopted...' (Chris Boogert, interim manager PMO of a retailer).

'We have introduced the Status Report in the programme. It has the big advantage that twenty projects are reported unambiguously. Thanks to the templates the project manager has to report briefly and concisely, where the most important milestones are continuously brought to the attention of the programme management. In the past a weekly report of thirty pages was not unusual' (controller, government authority).

In the next chapter I describe the PRINCE2 documents with reference to the building blocks. In Chapter 8 there are practical examples of these building blocks and the documents in which they are used.

3 The PRINCE2 documents

'To accomplish great things, we must not only act, but also dream; not only plan, but also believe.'
Anatole France, French novelist

In the previous chapter I explained how you can provide information systematically to stakeholders, without overfeeding them with bulky, inaccessible, standalone and illegible documents. The philosophy of building blocks and storyboarding was explained with reference to a number of PRINCE2 documents. This chapter provides an overview of the PRINCE2 documents and shows which PRINCE2 building blocks are used to build these documents up.

Document	No.	Sect.	PRINCE2 Process
Mandate	D1	3.1	Input to the process 'Starting up a project'
Business Case	D2	3.2	Implementation of the process 'Starting up a project'
Project Brief	D3	3.3	Implementation of the process 'Starting up a project'
			Input to the process 'Initiating a project'
Project Initiation Document (PID)	D4	3.4	Implementation of the process 'Initiating a project'
			Input to the process 'Directing a project'
			Input to the process 'Controlling a stage'
			Input to the process 'Managing product delivery'
			Input to the process 'Managing stage boundaries'
			Input to the process 'Closing a project'
Work Package	D5	3.5	Implementation of the process 'Controlling a stage'
			Input to the process 'Managing product delivery'
Status Report	D6	3.6	Implementation of the process 'Managing stage boundaries'
End Project Report	D7	3.7	Implementation of the process 'Closing a project'
Exceptions Report	D8	3.8	Implementation of the process 'Controlling a stage'
Lessons Report	D9	3.9	Implementation of the process 'Closing a project'
Issue Register	D10	3.10	Implementation of the process 'Controlling a stage'
Risk Register	D11	3.11	Implementation of the process 'Controlling a stage'
Lessons Learned Register	D12	3.12	Implementation of the process 'Controlling a stage'

Table 3.1　Relationship between PRINCE2 products and processes

3.1 Mandate (D1)

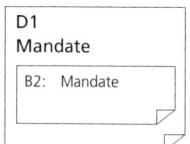

The Mandate document (D1) initiates the process 'Starting up a project'. The document consists of one building block: Mandate (B2). The responsibility for the mandate lies with the executive. The process 'Starting up a project' forms the foundation of the project. It precedes the actual project. The Mandate describes the essence of the project. It is the first building block of several documents. The Mandate describes the scope, the most important preconditions for the project and the relationship with other projects. Each follow-on document begins with this building block. For the reader it is immediately clear to which project the document refers. It is a useful tool for Project Board members in particular. They are often involved in several projects. See section 8.2 for a comprehensive example of the Mandate building block.

Concrete suggestions and practical tips
- Help the executive with the completion of the Mandate. The executive remains responsible for the Mandate of the future project.
- Make the objectives SMART (Specific, Measureable, Acceptable, Realistic and Timely).
- Ask what the underlying reason is when the executive indicates that a specific application or use is lacking and that the project should implement it. There may a simpler alternative.
- If there is not yet any project selection process, the Mandate is a useful tool for prioritizing projects. A discussion of Mandates can produce a ranking order.

3.2 Business Case (D2)

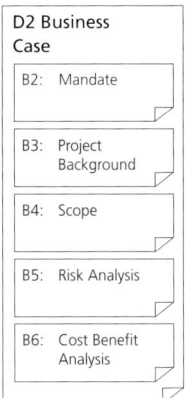

The Business Case is created during the 'Starting up a project' process. During the 'Initiating of a project' process the Business Case is developed further. The Business Case answers the following questions:

- Why are we starting the project?
- What are the advantages?
- What are the risks?
- What are the costs?

The answers to these questions provide an indication of the weight of the Business Case.

On the basis of the Business Case, the contribution of the project to the objectives of the organisation must become clear. Try to make it SMART: (Specific, Measurable, Acceptable, Realistic and Timely). The Business Case consists of five building blocks (see figure above).

Mandate (B2)
This was dealt with in the previous section.

Project Background (B3)
The Project Background describes – as the name indicates – the background to the project. Think, for example, of something such as a product that the market demands, an amendment to the law that requires an adaptation of systems, or a process in which disruptions or faults occur.

Scope (B4)
The Scope defines the delineation of the project. It is essential to review changes during the project. If the Scope is clear at the beginning of the project, all parties know what is and is not a part of the project. A clear Scope definition is useful to prevent improper changes ('scope creep'). The Scope describes the breadth of the project (for example the geographic areas of countries, the customer groups or products). The depth of the project is also important. Does the project only undertake an analysis of alternatives or are these options being developed and implemented?

Risk Analysis (B5)
This building block state the risk areas. Think about the business risk if delivery of the product is too late, the operational risk that the organisation runs when introducing a product, or the supplier's risk if external parties are necessary for the realization of the project. The scenario analysis determines the impact on the Business Case in terms of recovery time, costs and time to completion. To this end you can build scenarios for various risks, such as the extension of one month, six months or one year. Or you might consider the bankruptcy of a supplier. In addition the risk analysis mentions measures to minimize or limit risks.

Cost Benefit Analysis (B6)
This building block describes the cash flow of the project, the Net Present Value (NPV), the Internal Rate of Return (IRR), the payback period and the foundation of the costs and benefits. Only the outcomes of the analyses are recorded in this building block. Underlying detailed calculations are present, but are not a part of the Business Case. See section 8.6 for an explanation of the concepts mentioned.

Concrete suggestions and practical tips
- Always make the executive responsible for the Business Case of the future project. The project manager assists the executive in the completion and working out of the Business Case. He never takes responsibility for it, however.
- Agree on the depth to which the Business Case should be developed.
- Present only the total costs and benefits. The calculation details need not be shown.
- Distinguish corporate risks from project risks. Project risks are encountered within the project and have an effect on the project in terms of extension of the project, extra costs in the project, etc. The organisation runs a corporate risk if something happens to the project.
- See to it that the information presented can be understood by the Project Board.
- Regard every measure to limit a risk as a product. This product requires resources, a budget and a completion period.
- Cover all COPAFITJH aspects when determining risks (C=Commerce, O=Organisation, P=Processes, A=Administrative Organisation, F=Finances, I=Information, T=Technique, J=Judicial and H=Housing).

3.3 Project Brief (D3)

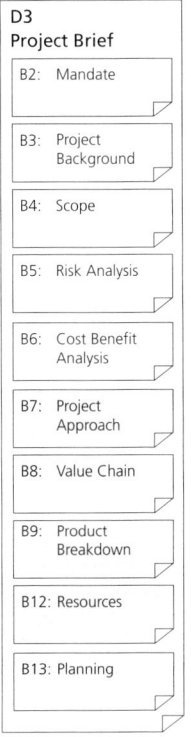

The final project management document in the process 'Starting up a project' is the Project Brief. This is a description of the proposed project in terms of the Business Case, the approach, the products, the planning and the resources. It forms the basis of the process 'Initiating a project'. The available Business Case (D2) is brought up to date and constructed using five additional building blocks.

Project Approach (B7)
This provides a visual representation of the steps in the project and the decisions taken in respect of the approach. Along with the decisions about the approach, the road not chosen is also described. With the development of an information system, you have for example the choice of in-house development or outsourcing. The description of the approach is useful to determine whether you can meet the expectations of the executive and other stakeholders. Suppose the executive had special requirements and the project proposed to select a standard off-the-shelf package, then it would be advisable to have a discussion about the project approach.

Value Chain (B8)
This building block provides a detailed account of the Value Chain (main processes) of the organisation. In the Value Chain all processes that the project possibly might be changing are flagged so that the executive can be clear about those processes that may impact upon the project.

Product Breakdown (B9)
The point of departure of PRINCE2 is product-based planning. The basis of this is the Product Breakdown or Breakdown Structure. This structure describes the most important intermediary and end products of the project. On the basis of the Breakdown, the project manager is able to do the planning of the delivery times of the (intermediary) products. The structure can also provide the basis for dividing the project into partial projects (per product cluster) and work packages (work to be done for an intermediary product).

The project team and the project manager determine the division that is suitable. The division must be simple and clear, and should not raise any new issues. The question of how far you should go with subdivision does not have a clear answer. If parts of a product are complex, or if high quality requirements are established, then a detailed subdivision into parts of the product will be necessary.

Resources (B12)
To be able to make decisions about the project, insight into the required resources is necessary. In the Project Brief, it is sufficient to provide a rough estimate of the type of job, the level of effort required and the general time frame when the people will be needed.

Planning (B13)
With this building block those concerned finally get an overall impression of the total planning of the project and a detailed view of the next process, 'Initiating the project'. The planning must be legible to the executive members and based on the products.

Concrete suggestions and practical tips
- Check on a regular basis within the organisation what opinions there are about the project approach.
- Do not go into more detail of the Project Breakdown than is necessary and useful for management of the project.
- Do not start with a project before the resources are available.
- Discuss their availability and motivation with possible project group members.
- Fine-tune the list of project group members with the executive.
- A condensed planning is sufficient. The project manager can work with a detailed plan, but this has less relevance for the Project Board.
- Record assumptions in the planning.
- Describe exceptions.
- Base the planning on the products, not on the activities.
- Record the milestones in the planning. Milestones are the points of measurement that indicate whether the project is still on track.
- Agree whether amounts should include or exclude VAT.

3.4 Project Initiation Document (PID)

The Project Initiation Document (PID) provides all the necessary information to the stakeholders involved in the project. The executive bases decisions about the starting of the project on the PID. For the project manager the PID can be compared to a contract, an agreement between the executive and the project manager. The contract describes the tolerances within which the project manager can operate (budget, time to completion, quality). The documents describe what expenses may be incurred for the products. The planned times are also described. In this way the PID provides the norm for reviewing changes and deciding how the project should continue. The PID is the end result of the process 'Initiating the project'. It consists of the actual project brief (D3). The PID is constructed by adding seven building blocks.

Organisation (B15)
This building block shows the organisational structure of the project. In each case the executive, the senior user and the senior supplier are represented on the Project Board. The project team consists of the project manager (reports to, but is not a member of the Project Board) and the project employees. The project manager can divide the products up amongst teams.

Budget details (B16)
This building block forms the basis for subsequent reporting on costs. In the PID this building block describes the budget needed to realize the project. This budget is subdivided into the following categories:

- Costs to be paid to third parties, such as:
  - external employees/consultants;
  - hardware/software;
  - travel and subsistence;
  - training;
  - other.

- Internal costs, such as:
  - internal employees.

Acceptance Criteria (B17)
This building block describes the acceptance criteria via which the executive will review the project. It gives the project manager insight into the aspects about which the executive will call him to account at the end of the project. It also provides protection to the project manager against requirements that were not known beforehand.

Architectural and Security Aspects (B18)
This building block contributes to harmony between the architectural and information security aspects of the project. It provides a summary of all the activities that have to be executed within the framework of architectural and information security. Think of activities like making an application landscape map or compiling an access control matrix.

Business Process Aspects (B19)
This building block provides a summary to those concerned of all activities within the frame of process adjustments. Think of process redesigning and of things like the requirements of the Sarbanes-Oxley SAS70 declaration, or regulatory bodies such as the Financial Markets Authority, the Nederlandsche Bank, etc. Similar regulations prescribe that checks should be incorporated within the processes, which indicate that work has been done in accordance with the process requirements.

Communication Plan (B20)
The communication plan describes what, how and when the project manager will communicate with the Project Board, the stakeholders and others involved. Think of possibilities like short news reports on the company intranet, presentations and the formal reporting occasions to the Project Board.

Quality Plan (B21)
This building block, in conclusion, describes for each product the quality requirements with which the product must comply, and who will be reviewing the product in terms of these requirements.

Concrete suggestions and practical tips
- Briefly describe the tasks, the qualifications and the responsibilities for each role.
- Draw up a project chart (stakeholders' analysis) and indicate what interests the players have in respect of the project (take account of users, interest groups (political), (external) advisers, project employees, line/staff management and hierarchical responsibilities).
- Leave all responsibilities to the Project Board members, as well as some PRINCE2 roles (Executive, Senior User, Senior Supplier) that have not been filled.
- Discuss the PID with fellow project managers before the executive gives his approval (peer review always enhances quality).
- See to it that the planning describes the processes and decision points (go/no go).
- Make an agreement with the executive to meet regularly for a cup of coffee. This provides the opportunity for sharing important issues immediately. It prevents surprises.
- Plan Project Board meetings in advance and clearly indicate these meetings in the planning. This is not in accordance with the PRINCE2 basic principle of 'Management by Exception'. However, practice shows that agendas are often overloaded. It is difficult to call a Project Board meeting at the last moment.
- In the final PID, deviations from the initial planning in the Project Brief should amount to no more than a maximum of 10%.

3.5 Work Package (D5)

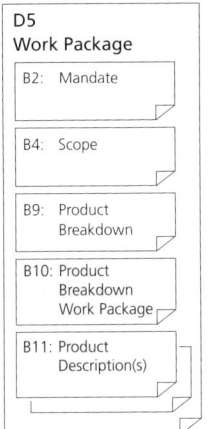

The creating of work packages happens during the process 'Initiating the project'. A work package provides the details of the products that are described in the PID (D4). Work packages also describe the agreements between the project manager and their team managers in respect of business products. Each work package consists of the building blocks Mandate, Scope and Product Breakdown. Through these the environment of the work package is clearly described. The Product Breakdown Work Package and the Product Description(s) complete the work package.

Product Breakdown Work Package (B10)
This building block is a further breakdown of the products in the work package. It shows the relationship between the parts of a product that are in the work package. A transaction processing system is, for example, built up out of three product parts: Transaction Input, Transaction Control and Transaction Processing. Based on the breakdown of the work package, the team manager is able to draw up a plan of the different (intermediary) products.

Product Description(s) (B11)
This building block provides a detailed description of each of the products, including the quality requirements with which it must comply. The quality requirements of the Transaction Input product are for example:

- maximum of one input screen;
- input fields are checked for validity;
- processing the transaction may last a maximum of 2 seconds.

The quality requirements for each individual product form a part of the overall quality requirements that are established for the products in the Project Initiation Document (D4).

Concrete suggestions and practical tips
- The work package is pre-eminently suited as a means of delegating tasks to a team manager or a project team member.
- Determine what knowledge and skills are required for the work packages.
- Determine what completion period is required.
- Make provision for an adequate margin.
- Come to definite agreements about the completion time of the work package.

3.6 The Status Report (D6)

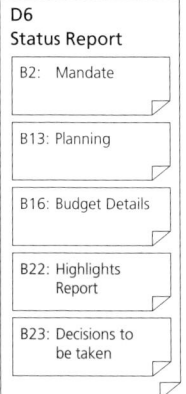

The Status Report is the instrument used to report to the Project Board. It shows to what extent the project is running according to plan. The Status Report consists of three building blocks from the PID (D4). In principle a Project Board report is produced at the end of a PRINCE2 stage. For practical reasons (agenda technical reasons in most organisations) the project managers sometimes opt for a publication frequency of once every three weeks or once per month. The meeting of the project group can be made dependent on possible decisions, so that the principle of 'Management by Exception' can be adhered to.

Due to these building blocks, meetings become efficient and effective. That is, the reporting is limited to the points decided on for the project. In this way content discussions are kept limited to a minimum.

Mandate (B2)
The content of the Mandate is, in principle, the same as in the PID. An important reason for change could be an alteration in the Scope or in one of the products.

Planning (B13)
The Planning also comes out of the PID (D4). It shows the progress in the realization of the various products. Here the Planning from the PID (D4) acts as the base case, so that the development, including the shifts, is visible.

Budget details (B16)
The budget is embedded in the PID. The Status Report describes the justification for the use of the allocated budget and the forecast of the costs. Figures must be coordinated with the controller. Correct figures show that the project manager has the project under control. In this building block the project manager can provide an analysis on the basis of the Earned Value. See section 8.16 for an explanation of this concept. The Status Report requires the project manager and the Project Board members to have sufficient knowledge of project financing.

The Status Report indicates the following categories (for all types of costs):

- costs incurred during the reporting period;
- total costs to date;
- costs still to be incurred up until the time of delivery;
- approved budget.

On the basis of these categories the following sections are derived:

- available capacity in the approved budget (approved budget - total costs to date) to compare with 'costs still to be incurred';
- forecast of the total costs (total costs + costs still to be incurred until time of delivery).

Comparison of the available budget and the costs still to be incurred gives Project Board members insight into the financial health of the project. The Earned Value Analysis (EVA) method is described in section 8.16.

Highlights Report (B22)
The Highlights Report provides a summary of the most important products and also indicates a traffic light for each product. This traffic light shows the progress of the product in respect of the planning. The Highlights Report describes traffic lights in respect of project planning, the budget, the resources, issues and the scope. In consultation with the executive, the report can be extended with particular traffic lights. Think, for example, of the integration of two departments where the executive periodically wants to know how satisfied the employees of the department are. If one of the traffic lights is on amber or red, there must be an issue that is the cause of this. The project manager explains for each issue what the consequences of the signal are and which measures they have taken.

Decisions to be taken (B32)
The last building block in the Status Report is 'decisions to be taken'. If the project runs according to expectations, there are no decisions. Should there be a proposed decision, the consequences in terms of changes to the budget, planning, scope and resources are described. If there are more decisions to be taken, this building block will occur several times in the Status Report.

Concrete suggestions and practical tips
- If no decisions are required, it is not necessary for the Project Board to meet (the 'Management by Exception' principle of PRINCE2).
- Only report on products ensuing from the Product Breakdown.
- The product manager directs by focusing on timely delivery of products. The executive directs by focusing on decision points.
- As an alternative to the indication of stoplights in the Highlights Report, the acronym OTOBOS (On Time, On Budget, On Scope) can be used.

3.7 End Project Report (D7)

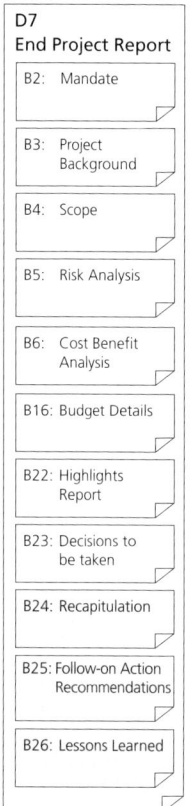

This document is the concluding product of the project. The project manager describes the delivered products in this document. In addition, the End Project Report provides a means of comparison with the Planning, the Budget and the Quality Requirements that are stated in the PID (D4). On the basis of this, the project manager provides an update on the Business Case (D2). Finally, a record is made in the End Project Report of when any remaining issues will be completed. To build up the End Project Report, two building blocks have been added to the building blocks that are already available: Recapitulation and Follow-on Action Recommendations.

Recapitulation (B24)
Through the use of the Recapitulation building block those concerned get an overview of the products that were planned to be delivered and actual products delivered. It explains which products the project has not delivered, or has correctly delivered, in addition to those specified in the PID. In addition Recapitulation provides a comparison of the actual budget and the time to completion with the original budget and completion time.

Follow-on Action Recommendations (B25)
This building block provides a summary of all outstanding issues, risks and recommendations. It details who is responsible for the completion of each outstanding item . In addition the project manager can put in a proposal for the post-project review (who prepares it, when it will be done, who will be involved?).

After approval of the End Project Report and the Lessons Report (D9) (see section 3.9), the project manager is relieved of their responsibility for the project. If there is no separate Lessons Report, the incorporation of the Lessons Learned building block (B26) in the End Project Report suffices.

Lesson Learned (B26)
This building block describes the strong points, the weak points and the lessons learned during the project.

Concrete suggestions and practical tips
- Discuss the End Project Report with fellow project managers. This enhances cooperation, contributes to exchange of knowledge and improves quality.
- Celebrate successes. Reward the commitment of project team members.
- Pass on all project documentation.

3.8 Exceptions Report (D8)

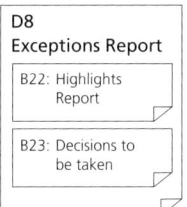

The Exceptions Report describes the exceptions. With reference to an analysis (including the effect on budget, planning and quality) it shows alternative ways of addressing a situation. The Exceptions Report consists of two building blocks.

Highlights Report (B22)
The Highlights Report shows what the problem is. A problem is a deviation from the desired situation, such as exceeding the planning, the budget or the tolerances that have been agreed upon (in the PID).

Decisions to be taken (B32)
This building block describes the decisions to be taken, possible alternatives and the consequences for the planning, the budget and the scope of the project.

After a decision has been made and an alternative chosen by the Project Board, the project manager adjusts the original budget, the completion time and the scope accordingly. Henceforth the project manager will report on exceptions in respect of these new (approved) particulars.

Concrete suggestions and practical tips
- 'Do nothing' is an alternative (nil-option).
- Indicate your own preferences for the alternatives.
- Commit on a course of action. Consensus is not always feasible and advisable.
- Walk the walk and talk the talk.

3.9 Lessons Report (D9)

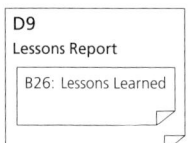

This is a document that describes all lessons learned arising out of the project. After the Project Board has approved the Lessons Report, the document is available for use in future projects.

The project manager can add the Lessons Report as a building block to the End Project Report (D7) or present it as an independent document. Based on the strong and weak points of the project, lessons are obtained that can be applied to future projects.

If the Lessons Report is an independent document, the following is a useful breakdown:

- project management;
- requirements;
- scope;
- change control;
- interfaces;
- realization;
- testing;
- data conversion;
- after-care;
- infrastructure/technology.

Stakeholders formulate the lessons learned, based on weak and strong points.

> Concrete suggestions and practical tips
> - Discuss the Lessons Report with fellow project managers. This enhances collaboration, contributes to exchange of knowledge and improves quality.
> - Collect the Lessons Reports of different projects and group comparable lessons learned together. Draw conclusions and make recommendations.

The PRINCE2 documents that relate to the formal decision points (go and no-go) in the project, and the PRINCE2 processes relating to directing and closure have been described in the previous sections. Think of the PID as the result of the process, 'Initiating a project'. After a formal decision, the PID becomes the basis for directing all processes. In addition to these process and time-restricted documents, PRINCE2 has the following log books that the project manager updates and monitors during the entire project life cycle:

- Issue Register;
- Risk Register;
- Lessons Learned Register.

3.10 Issue Register (D10)

This log contains a list of issues (problems, new requirements and lapsed requirements). The description of each issue includes an explanation, manner of assessment, establishment of priorities, decisions taken and explanation of the current status. The project manager assesses the Issue Register. Closure or reporting issues can only be done in consultation with the project manager. At the start of the project the project manager negotiates process agreements (Change Control or Change Procedure) in respect of handling changes (issues).

3.11 Risk Register (D11)

The Risk Register is an expanding document. The log consists of a summary of all known risks, the possibility of these occurring, their likely impact, measures taken to reduce the individual risks and the responsibility for managing these risks. Insight and overview are fundamental to successful risk management. The project manager is responsible for the Risk Register. He records the initial risks in the Business Case. The project manager updates the Risk Register during the project. 'Consider that the greatest problems lie where we are not looking for them' (freely translated from W. von Goethe, 1749-1832).

3.12 Lessons Learned Register (D12)

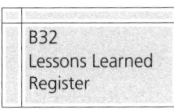

This is an expanding document in which the project manager records all the lessons learned during the project. These are situations or decisions that accelerate or hamper the project. It is recommended that the divisions of the Lessons Report (D9) are used when preparing the layout of the log. Suppose that the Lessons Report is subdivided into the focal areas of project management, requirements and realization. With the lessons learned shown in the log, you would indicate whether a specific lesson learned relates to project management, requirements or realization.

Concrete suggestions and practical tips
- Agree on who will keep the logs up to date.
- Constantly update the logs.
- Make use of simple aids (for example a spreadsheet).

3.13 Summary

In this chapter I have described all documents in the PRINCE2 product model. The building blocks that make up each document have been explained. In the following two chapters I will indicate, with reference to PRINCE2, which building blocks play a role in the PRINCE2 themes and in a number of techniques. In e.g. the PRINCE2 theme, Organisation, all building blocks are brought into play where decisions are made in respect of organisation and resources. In this way you can make the connection between the building blocks that are described and the application of PRINCE2 in your own organisation.

4 Relationship with the PRINCE2 themes

'When spider webs unite, they can tie up a lion'.
African proverb

In addition to processes, PRINCE2 also has so-called themes. The project manager uses these themes in the execution of the processes and in organizing and directing their project. The themes are indicated in the following table.

Themes	No.	Sect.	Related Building Blocks
Business Case[5]	Th1	4.1	B2, B3, B4, B5, B6
Organisation	Th2	4.2	B1, B2, B12, B15, B22, B24
Planning	Th3	4.3	B13, B22
Progress Assessment	Th4	4.4	B5, B6, B16, B22, B23, B25
Risk Management	Th5	4.5	B2, B5, B14, B22, B25, B30, B31
Quality in projects	Th6	4.7	B11, B17, B21, B22
Change Management	Th7	4.8	B1, B22, B23, B30, B31

Table 4.1   Relationship between PRINCE2 themes and building blocks

The following sections show the connection between the PRINCE2 themes and the building blocks. In addition I make use of the concept of storyboarding (or story-line) from the film industry as previously explained in section 2.3. By means of referring to the story-line, the consistency between different documents can be shown. All building blocks where e.g. project organisation and resources are mentioned must be in line with each other, otherwise there is a mistake in one of the documents. The storyboard describes the logical coherence.

4.1   Business Case (Th1)

Every project must contribute to the objectives of an organisation. One of the cornerstones of PRINCE2 is the Business Case. In section 3.2 I describe the building blocks which are used to build up the Business Case. The Business Case provides answers to four questions:

- why are we starting the project?
- what are the advantages and benefits?
- what are the risks during the execution?
- what are the costs?

---

[5] PRINCE2 speaks about the Business Case in two ways. On the one hand as a sub-section (product part) of the Project Brief (D3) and the PID (D4), and on the other hand as a theme that supports the project manager in the different processes.

Based on these answers the executive makes decisions about the project. During the execution (when there is a change in scope, budget or completion time) and when managing stage boundaries, the executive has to review the Business Case once more. If the Business Case is no longer deemed positive, they will stop the project.

The following diagram indicates the relationship between the building blocks described and the four questions.

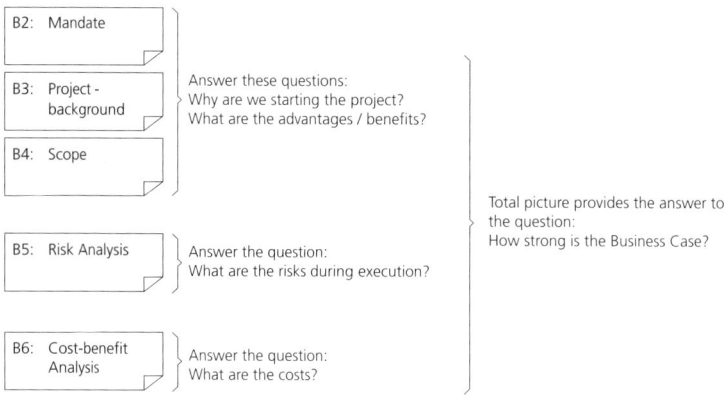

Figure 4.1   Relationship between Business Case and building blocks

At the start of the project there is generally a rudimentary Business Case. Top management uses this justification in the (bi)annual project portfolio management process[6]. In this process the management makes choices in respect of the projects placed on the list of projects to be realized. The executive is the owner of the Business Case and, as a consequence, is responsible for its correctness. The project manager may help to draw up the Business Case. During the project, the project manager becomes responsible for the assessment of the Business Case. After the project is completed it is again the responsibility of the executive to actually achieve the budgeted advantages and benefits.

4.2   Organisation (Th2)

Within a project it must be clear to all stakeholders what is expected of them. The arrangement of the project organisation (Project Board, project group, work groups) is important. The various tasks, competences and responsibilities are described in the following sections.

4.2.1   Structure

The point of departure of PRINCE2 is the relationship between the executive and project manager or client and supplier. The client or executive commissions someone to undertake the project.

---

[6] Project Portfolio Management: The process by which, on the basis of an analysis, projects are chosen that contribute most to the corporate objectives.

They reap the fruits of the result. The contractor or supplier realizes (produces) the products. PRINCE2 distinguishes between the project manager and the subject matter expert. The project manager handles the management of the project and the subject matter expert creates the content that makes up the products.

PRINCE2 has various management levels: The Project Board (decision body consisting of the Executive, the Senior User and the Senior Supplier), the project manager and possibly team managers. The project manager and the Project Board can set up advice and sounding-board groups. These groups have no decision powers, but it is sometimes advisable to enlarge the basis and so provide the facility for explaining expectations.

4.2.2 Story-line project organisation and resources

What does directing of a project look like, who is involved with the project, and how do you know when someone makes a contribution to the project? These are all questions to which the executive, according to PRINCE2, must supply answers at the beginning of the project and which the executive will continually check during the execution. The story-line is described below.

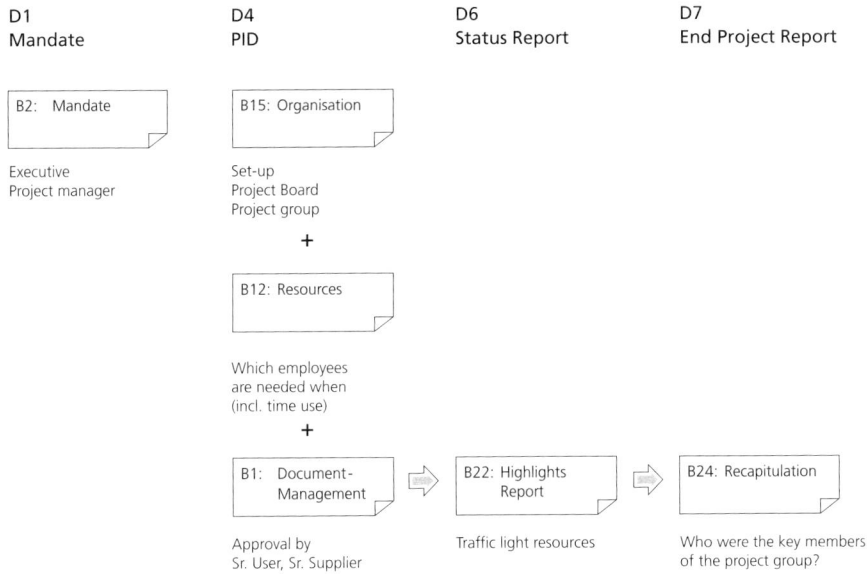

Figure 4.2   Project organisation and resources

The responsibility for the Mandate (D1) lies with the executive. By means of the Mandate the executive shows the proposed project manager what the intention of the assignment is. A summary of the stakeholders is included in the Mandate. Consultation between the project manager and the executive then provides the outlines for the project organisation structure contained in the PID (D4). The relevant roles are clarified and the corresponding tasks, competences and responsibilities are divided up. In the project group three roles are represented:

- the Executive: The owner of the Business Case and budget controller. The executive puts the question: 'Are the costs in proportion to the benefits?'
- the Senior User: They assess the suitability of the result within the organisation. Will it work?
- the Senior Supplier: They are responsible for the delivery of the experts and the materials/tools for the execution of the project. They put the question: 'Can we make it?'

The Resources building block (see section 8.12) describes the employees required for the project. It ensures that within the composition of the team, the individual qualities of the employees are known. The success of the project begins with the success of the team members. A useful aid here would be the team roles of Belbin (2006) or the Enneagram (Riso, 2005). In situations where the employees are allocated to a project and the project manager is not able to make a choice, it is recommended that the lack of any specialist knowledge or skills is highlighted as a risk and discussed with the Project Board.

For the following stage of the project, the names of the resources must be known. The support of the executive staff is essential to ensure the commitment of their employees. If such support is lacking, then it would be wise to highlight this as a project risk and to allocate responsibility for these resources to one of the Project Board members.

4.2.3 Key Process Indicator

Within organisations I often come across a small group of employees (key figures) who are always involved in projects. Their lack of availability poses a potential risk to the projects they are participating in. In order to address this, it is recommended that a Key Process Indicator (KPI) is stated in the Highlights Report of the project (see section 8.22). This KPI describes the issues in the project regarding the resources (to be filled in according to the RAG status generally applied: Red, Amber, Green):

- red: there is a problem. The project manager compiles an Exceptions Report on behalf of the project group. Options that the Project Board may consider are: do less, deliver later, lower the quality, add more people;
- amber: there is a potential problem. The project manager expects to be able to solve this themselves (re-planning, closer consultation with the line manager, replacement, etc.);
- green: no problems.

In addition to the availability (or more precisely, the absence) of key staff members, the project manager can encounter other people-related problems in their project:

- overloading (too many tasks for one employee);
- under-burdening (too little work for one employee);
- internal conflicts;
- over-familiarity (resulting in covering up mistakes);
- incorrect role assignment (overlapping);
- motivation;
- over-enthusiasm.

With the closure of the project the Recapitulation building block (see section 8.24) shows who the key staff members for the project were. This provides the opportunity, if appropriate, to seek to involve these people once again in similar projects.

4.3 Planning (Th3)

When must the project team develop the products (parts) in order to deliver the requested end product? PRINCE2 has an overall project plan for the entire project and a detailed plan for every stage. The PID (D4) describes the overall project plan. For this you should refer to the Planning building block (section 8.13). At the end of a stage the project manager provides a detailed plan for the next stage. Readjustments of the overall project plan are then made, as necessary. They report on the status of the planning in the Highlights Report. A detailed stage plan is also drawn up for the compiling of the PID.

4.4 Progress Assessment (Th4)

Progress Assessment makes it possible to take decisions at the correct points in time. Reporting on the progress and the exceptions provides the opportunity for reducing the risk of exceeding time and budget. Control begins with the handling of fundamental PRINCE2 principles. The most important is the taking of *go/no-go* decisions based on the Business Case. This constitutes a part of the Project Brief (D3) and the PID (D4). Control based on the Exceptions Report (D8) and the Highlights Report (B22) occurs during the execution of the project.

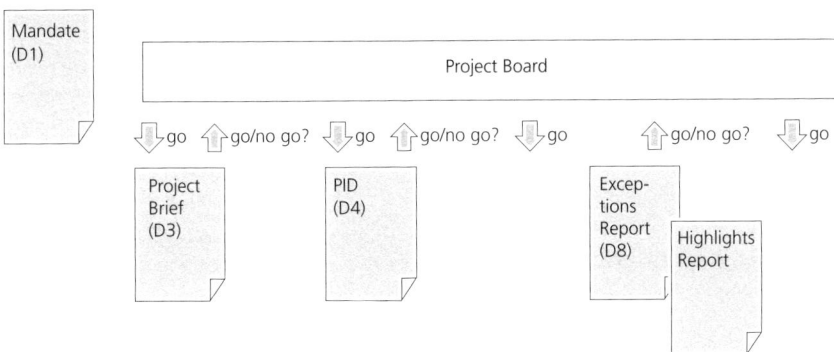

Figure 4.3 Go/no-go decisions

The project manager describes the status of the planning, the budget, the resources and the scope with KPI's. A traffic light (RAG status) illustrates any exceptions in relation to the agreements set out in the PID (D4). In my opinion the control of the finances is an important role set aside for the financial department. I shall flesh this out in the next section.

4.4.1 'In control' with the financial department

In my opinion the authority of the controller of the financial department is not given sufficient voice in PRINCE2 in respect of projects. The possibility exists of the financial department being scarcely involved at all, and this poses an extra risk. What information is necessary to enable the financial department to provide an 'in control' statement of the reported costs of the projects that are running?

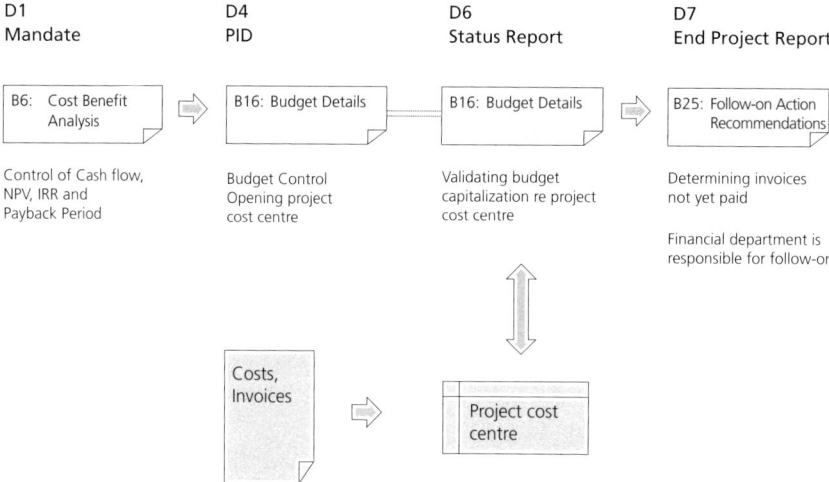

Figure 4.4 'In control' with the financial department

In order to allow the financial department to provide appropriate controls in an efficient and effective way, it is necessary to present the required information in an identifiable and concise manner. The PRINCE2 method has not defined the role of the controller clearly. A comparison of the project cost centre with the budget contained in the Status Report (D6) provides a means by which the financial department can contribute.

All consultations between the project manager and the controller can be traced back to the creation and validation of the project management documents (see Figure 4.4). What exactly was stated in the agenda during these consultations is described in the next story-line.

When doing the cost benefit analysis (a part of the Business Case), the controller reviews the calculation of the Net Present Value (NPV), the Internal Rate of Return (IRR) and the payback period. He ensures that all projects operate from the same points of departure, such as the interest rate and the hourly rate. This control makes prioritization possible on the basis of the Business Case (project portfolio process). This review also makes it possible for the financial department to calculate the effect of the changes in operational costs (staff, hardware and software) and benefits throughout the entire organisation budget.

A sub-section of the PID (D4) is the Budget building block (B16). This building block is the basis for the financial report. The Budget building block describes the expected external (out-of-pocket) and the internal costs.

When the Project Board has approved the PID (D4), it is the trigger for the controller to open a project cost centre. This cost centre describes all out-of-pocket costs (invoices). The controller can now provide insight into the financial situation of the project 'with a single push of a button'. The project manager no longer needs to spend too much time on this. The controller is able to fulfil their role in the project, and everybody knows what the current financial status is.

The budget traffic light (costs KPI) in the Highlights Report can be compared with other traffic lights. It illustrates the quality of the financial status and has three positions:

- red: there is an overspending that can no longer be redeemed. The Project Board gets an Exceptions Report;
- amber: the budget utilisation is not running according to plan, but it is expected to recover;
- green: the budget utilisation is running according to plan.

The Status Report (D6) gives an account of the progress of the project to the Project Board. The Status Report shows the utilization of the funds. The controller has the task of comparing the budget with the entries in the project cost centre before the publication of the Status Report. In the event of an exception, an analysis of the difference is done. The exception results in a change to the budget or the cost centre.

The End Project Report (D7) provides the closing report of the project manager to the Project Board. In addition to the updated Business Case and the final Status Report, it describes two building blocks, namely the Recapitulation and the Follow-on Action Recommendations. The planned and delivered products rest on the Recapitulation building block. In addition, the actual and the original planning as well as the budget are reflected visually (including reasons for differences). Here the financial department is also required to compare the budget with the project cost centre beforehand. The project manager incorporates the Follow-on Action Recommendations and the outstanding invoice amount in the End Project Report. The financial department supervises the payment of these invoices. In addition, the project manager specifies all outstanding issues and risks together with the related responsibilities. After approval of the End Project Report the project manager is released from their commitments.

The proposed procedure contributes to the involvement of the controller by enabling them to be 'in control' of the financial aspect of projects. The controller becomes involved with the creation and validation of all building blocks that have a financial aspect. In this way a better guarantee of the financial reliability of projects is achieved.

4.4.2 Transfer to maintenance and operation

It holds true for every project that the world does not end with the closure of that project. When the products have been delivered, the organisation still has to operate and maintain these products. To operate products, the organisation has to make knowledge available. Here again, it is a task for the project manager. The project manager provides the maintenance and operational documents at the end of the project. These are content documents that are dependent on the underlying product and the organisation. I will describe these in outline.

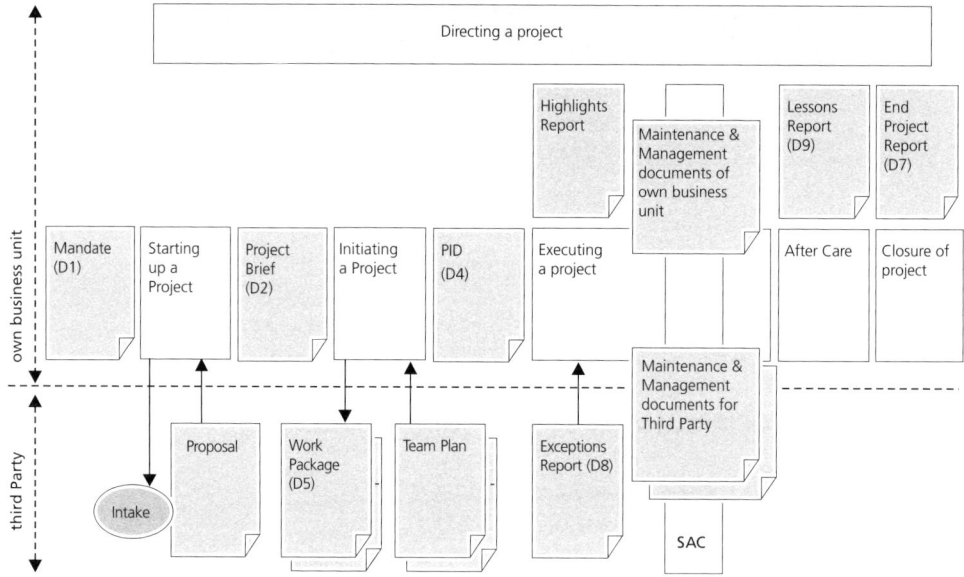

Figure 4.5 Maintenance and operational documents

I call the maintenance and operational documents the Service Acceptance Checklist (SAC). PRINCE2 doesn't recognizes this. The SAC describes documents of a technical and functional nature, namely Service Level Agreements, contracts and operational instructions. Agreements in respect of all documents are to be put in place (in the form of work packages) during the process 'Initiating a project'. Only then does it become clear who is responsible for providing these documents, which requirements apply and what the costs might be.

4.5   Risk Management (Th5)

In addition to actual planning, up-to-date Risk and Issue Registers are crucial for the managing of projects. Moreover, these logs are important when handing over documents, should it be necessary to replace the project manager.

The Mandate (B2) is the first building block in which the risks and issues are incorporated. This is done in the form of limitations, preconditions and relationships with other projects. Determining the risks and the accompanying risk analysis is a logical follow-on step after the analysis of the Mandate. This condition forms a part of the Business Case. The Risk Register is completed further during the process 'Initiating the project'. Next the different risks are stated in the PID (Risk Building Block B14). During the project the project manager keeps the Risk and Issue Registers up to date. At the start of the project the project manager enters into agreements with the Project Board about the handling of changes and issues (Change Control procedure). The status of the issues can be seen in the Highlights Report. The KPI for issues is reflected by the well-known (RAG) traffic light colours:

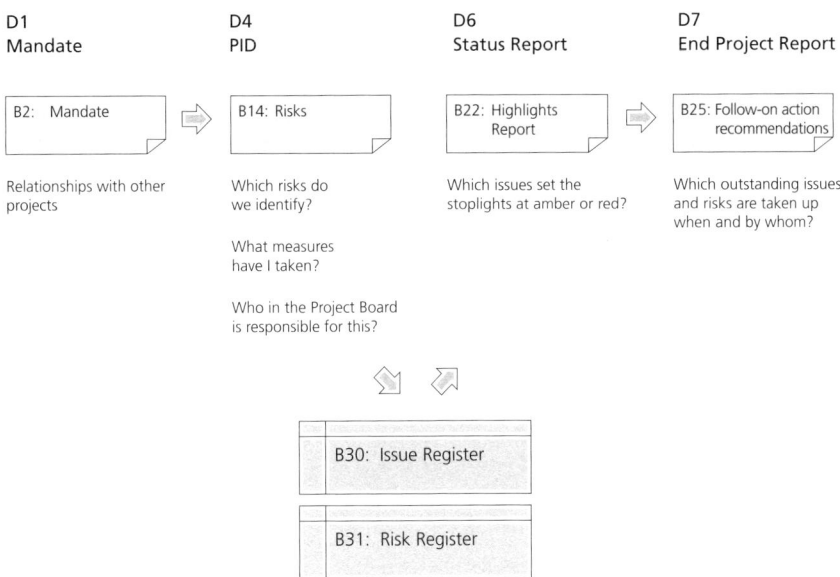

Figure 4.6 Risks and Issues

- red: issues are endangering the project. An Exceptions Report is prepared for the Project Board;
- amber: issues are endangering the project, but the project manager expects to be able to resolve these themself;
- green: no issues are endangering the project (in terms of planning, budget and scope).

With the closure of the project, the End Project Report provides a summary of all the issues and risks that are still unresolved. This summary also indicates who is responsible for this. This is described in the building block Follow-on Action Recommendations (B25).

In the *Harvard Business Review* (September 2007), a fascinating method of identifying risks (the so-called project pre-mortem) is described. At the beginning of the project a session is convened in which failures of the project constitute the point of departure. Everybody is asked to indicate what went wrong. All the participants then write down reasons for the failures of the project. Each reason (one per person) is individually reviewed. The project manager compiles a complete list and then searches for ways of enhancing his plan, for he is now able to prevent the reasons provided in every instance.

4.6 Quality in projects (Th6)

In PRINCE2 the quality of the project is central. Ultimately the products must meet the fixed requirements. In the following sections the quality assessment of the products, the quality assessment of the project management documents and the quality assessment between projects are addressed.

4.6.1 Quality assessment of the products

Without going at length into the quality of the products, I want to stress that various building blocks contain descriptions of the associated qualities. With the Acceptance Criteria the executive indicates the conditions upon which they accept the results of the project. The building block Quality Plan (B21) describes the valid quality requirements and the checking of the requirements for all products. The building blocks for the Product Description describe for each product (part), amongst other things, the quality criteria, the quality method and the responsibility for the reviewing of these criteria. These quality reviews can result in issues. If these issues have come about before the planning of the budget, then we would see them again in the Highlights Report (B22). In this case the Project Board would react accordingly to these issues. The Project Board is responsible for guaranteeing the quality. Refer to section 5.2 for more details on the technique of quality checks.

4.6.2 Quality assessment of project management documents

All products must comply with fixed quality requirements. These requirements apply to all projects within an organisation. They are not stipulated separately in the PID (D4). Compliance with the described documentation standard calls for a quality assessor. If there is a Project Management Office (PMO) within the organisation, this function can fulfill the role of quality assessor. The PMO reports periodically to the management on the quality of the project management documents.

The use of, and testing by means of story-lines guarantees consistency between and within project management documents. The project manager can do this, or a quality reviewing body such as the Project Management Office, as described above. In this role the PMO supervises:

- use of standard building blocks;
- provision of project management documents (the minimum applying to all projects is that the Mandate (D1), the PID (D4) and the End Project Report (D7) must be provided);
- use of the archiving standard;
- use of naming conventions.

Stated exceptions can result in an adjustment of the standard. If the project manager lacks the required knowledge, then an appropriate training course can provide a solution.

With the closure of the project, care must also be taken to provide a complete and relevant archive and to move this archive to the closed projects directory. Bos and Haiting (2007) test the quality of an archive in terms of the following aspects:

- accessibility;
- completeness;
- redundancy;
- topicality.

4.6.3 Quality assessment between projects

A simple aid to assess the consistency and the dependencies between projects is the Highlights Report (B22). If one project is dependent upon a product of another project, the KPI's in respect of planning must correspond. In this situation the PMO can play a role. The PMO can apply resourceful techniques, such as the use of *walls* and *stand-up meetings*. An example is the weekly collection and pasting up of all Highlights Reports of projects on a wall. A stand-up meeting in front of this wall provides project managers with the opportunity to discuss the status of their respective projects. They share relevant information and the connection between projects becomes visible.

4.7 Change Management (Th7)

Change Management takes care of the assessment and the controlled implementation of changes in products. One of the causes for project failure is known as *scope creep*. Scope creep results in project extension or budget overrun. The cause is often to be found in the Change Authority that has been set up inadequately (or not at all) with correspondingly inadequate processes. In consultation with the executive, the project manager agrees on where the authority for changes lies. The Project Board is usually responsible, but there can also be a separate Change Authority. The Change Authority gives permission for the implementation of changes. If it is a separate body, it is advisable to incorporate a separate Change Budget in the project budget. In this way the financial responsibilities are clear.

The handling of changes during the execution of a project determines its success. If you review changes separately, the consequences for the project in terms of the scope, budget and completion period remain controllable. Change Control is intended to fulfil this purpose. Without Change Control projects can get out of hand very quickly. With a change in the specifications of the acceptance criteria of a product (the so-called *Requests for Changes* - RfC's) structured completion is possible. In addition to change requests, changes can also arise as a result of mistakes (*Off-specification*).

4.8 Summary

In this chapter I have described the PRINCE2 themes and fleshed out the relationship with the building blocks. In addition I have illustrated how story-lines can be an instrument to guarantee and assess the consistency between building blocks and the PRINCE2 documents. In the following chapter a number of techniques and their relationship with building blocks get an airing. I deal with the various techniques using the same system of story-lines.

5 Relationship with the techniques

'Those who are skilled in combat do not become angered.
Those who are skilled at winning do not become afraid.
Thus the wise win before the fight, while the ignorant fight to win'.
Aikido proverb.

In Chapter 4 we looked at the relationship between the building blocks and the themes in PRINCE2. This chapter deals with the usefulness of the building blocks for different techniques.[7] The techniques as such are dealt with very briefly. The accent lies on the actual use of the building blocks.

Techniques	No.	Sect.	Related Building Blocks
Product-Based Planning	T1	5.1	B2, B4, B9, B10, B11, B13, B21, B24
Quality Checks	T2	5.2	B11, B17, B21
Configuration Management	T3	5.3	All building blocks
Lessons Learned and Client Satisfaction	T4	5.4	B26, B28, B29, B32

Table 5.1 Relationship between techniques and building blocks

5.1 Product-Based Planning (T1)

This technique provides the specifications for the products. The project planning is based on these products. Through this, the executive knows when the products are to be delivered.

Figure 5.1 shows the documents for product-based planning and the matching building blocks. The Mandate (B2) is the starting point for the Status Report (D6). The Mandate provides a summary of the most important products. The Scope building block then describes the boundaries for each product. The Scope building block provides the breadth and the depth of the project (from the preliminary study through to completion).

The Product Breakdown (B10) analyses the products in terms of product parts. If you then determine the quality requirements for these products, you have the basis for the planning. A plan that is based on the Product Breakdown shows the sequence of the project activities. The delivery data of the various products constitutes the starting point of the Highlights Report (B22). With the Highlights Report, the project manager can periodically provide an update of the state of affairs in respect of the status of the products.

In conclusion, the Recapitulation Building Block (B24) in the End Project Report (D7) provides a summary of the requested and delivered products.

---

[7] A number of techniques are described in PRINCE2™ version 2005. In the 2009 version, references to other OGC products have been included. For the sake of providing continuity with the previous Dutch edition of this book and the relationship with the building blocks, the techniques have been included in this book as well.

Figure 5.1 Building blocks for product-based planning

Should there be comparable projects within the organisation, the project manager can make use of templates for the Product Breakdown. These templates describe the experiences gained with earlier projects. The use of such templates saves the person involved time and improves the accuracy:

- design templates for tasks and projects that occur regularly;
- design and process templates with reference to project evaluations;
- use a template at the point of departure, not at the finishing point;
- adapt templates on the basis of project evaluations.

5.2 Quality Check (T2)

The Quality Check is a technique to judge whether a product meets the specified quality requirements. At the start of the project it is determined who will be carrying out these checks. The quality expectations of the executive are laid down in the Acceptance Criteria (B17) of the PID (D4). In the Work Packages (D5) these quality criteria are developed further for each product. In addition, the measuring method to be adopted for the criteria is also described. It is further detailed who will review the criteria (see Figure 5.2).

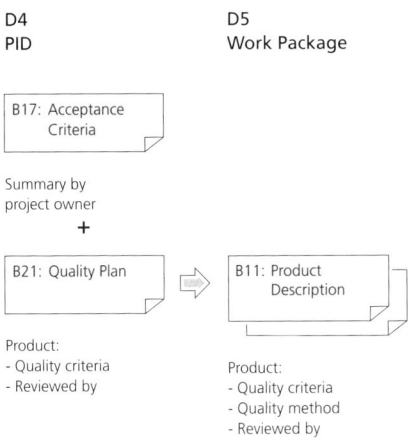

Figure 5.2   Building blocks for quality checks

In projects the planned reviews are a good instrument for checking the quality of products. Checking by means of quality criteria makes it possible to determine the level of completeness and to guarantee the relationship with other products. It is an instrument to establish with certainty that the product complies with all requirements.

5.3   Configuration Management (T3)

Configuration Management comprises the identifying, registering and recording (archiving) of all components, such as documents and products (parts). The version of every component is shown, together with an indication of which is the current version.

It is recommended to establish an 'environment' where the project management documents can be organised and stored. The archiving of project documents, such as the corporate requirements, the recording of the processes and procedures, the analysis and design (functional, technical) as well as the decision documents, is very important. The primary purpose for archiving is to assist in the retrieval and reproduction of the project management documents and the project products. Other motives for archiving are for project continuity, and provision of evidence in any future (legal) conflicts.

In summary, configuration management makes it possible to use the statistics acquired through experience and products, and lessons learned in other projects.

The classification of an archive must be clear. Think, for example, of a main division that distinguishes between current projects and closed projects. For each individual project various subdivisions can be set up in relation to the stages of the project, project management documents and content documents. The following classification provides an example:

Project n
- Products
  - Stage z
- Project management
  - General
  - Correspondence (all project-related memos and letters)
  - Discussions
  - Progress (Status Report and Highlights Reports)
  - Initiation (Mandate, Project Brief, PID)
  - Quality products (Action List, Risk Register and Issue Register)
  - Evaluation (Lessons Learned Register)
  - Finances (Budget calculation, summary for the benefit of the Status Report)
- Work in progress
  - Product n and stage z
  - Project employees
    * Name 1
    * Name n
  - Other

The above division is based around content. Other division styles can be based on alphabetical order or time sequence. In these divisions it may be difficult to retrieve a document if the exact name of the document or the production date is not known.

The corporate intranet can be used to publish a variety of documents. Publication of standards in an accessible medium such as the corporate intranet enlarges the communication platform. In addition it is practical to publish the Mandate (D1) at the start of a project and the Lessons Report (D9) at the closure of a project via the corporate intranet.

When naming documents the following aspects play an important role:

- belongs to: project, standard, etc.;
- document type: PID, Highlights Report, End Project Report, etc.;
- date created: if the date begins with the day, it is awkward to do a search via, for example, Windows Explorer, with the result that the sequence of the documents can get mixed up;
- sorting: documents that belong together are placed together;
- version: documents are adapted in the course of time, so having a version number immediately indicates clearly that it is an older document.

The application of the above aspects results in a simple naming convention. In this way everybody can find the required document.

Project name (document type, yyyymmdd) version number

With the application of this convention to a project named GAMMA, the PID and the Highlights Report would be allocated the following names:

GAMMA (Highlights Report, 20060410) V1.0
GAMMA (Highlights Report, 20060417) V1.0
GAMMA (PID, 20060416) V1.0

And the documentation standard:

PMO (standard building blocks, 20070112) V3.2

> Concrete suggestions and practical tips
> - In addition to the project archiving, it is recommended that the standard of documentation is documented as well.

5.4 Lessons Learned and Customer Satisfaction (T4)

During the project, the project manager records all strong and weak points in the Lessons Learned Register (B32). These points form the basis of the Lessons Report (D9). Depending on the size of the project, the Lessons Learned building block (B26) in the End Project Report can suffice, or a separate document can be created.

The project manager submits a draft Lessons Report to all members of the project team and the Project Board for their comments. After the Project Board has approved the report, it is made available for new projects.

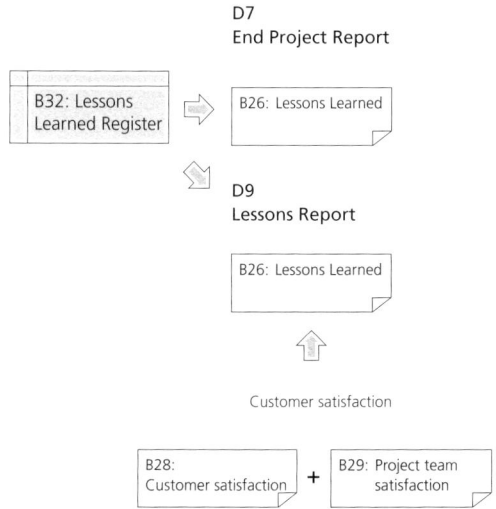

Figure 5.3   Lessons learned and customer satisfaction

Depending on the size of the organisation and the number of projects undertaken, discussion of the lessons learned with fellow project managers may be possible. It is useful to share and disseminate experiences. In this way a process of improvement is created.

In addition to the log of the project manager, feedback from the organisation is a valuable source of lessons learned. The stakeholders and the project team members give feedback at the closure of the project. They review the following aspects:

- the degree to which the objective has been achieved;
- the approach and procedure used;
- the input of the project manager.

The most important players in the project team review the following aspects:

- project structure and organisation;
- planning and assessment;
- budget assessment;
- management style;
- communication.

5.5   Summary

In this chapter I have described a number of techniques and fleshed out the relationship with the building blocks. In addition I have illustrated how story-lines can be used as tools to guarantee consistency between the building blocks and the PRINCE2 documents. The following chapter is an interlude, which deals with the developments and trends in the use of information systems for document management. Chapter 7 then goes on to describe the introduction of the storyboard and building block concept.

6 Developments and trends

*'A tool cannot replace a method,
it can only help in carrying it out'.*

I have not discussed the potential use of complex information systems for handling the building blocks in the preceding chapters. The use of the familiar office automation tools will generally suffice for these building blocks. These tools are capable of establishing and keeping the information and project management processes under control. Once the processes have been established, the organisation can take follow-on steps, such as the introduction of an information system for project portfolio management (PPM). The project management will then have come of age. The corporate risk as a result of project failure is reduced. The subsequent steps in professionalizing project management are: optimizing the use of the corporate resources and introduction of programme management.

Portfolio management speaks for itself. Think of making the status of projects insightful. Practice has shown that there is a limit to the number of projects that an organisation can execute simultaneously. It is advisable to be selective. Portfolio management provides the processes for this. If your organisation is ready for the next step on the 'project management maturity ladder', the implementation of project and portfolio tools can be considered.

6.1 Project and portfolio management systems

Gartner has done a lot of research regarding information systems and tools. Figure 6.1 shows that suppliers such as CA Clarity (formerly Niku), HP PPM, Microsoft Project, Primavera, Plan View and Compuware are the market leaders in terms of supplying project and portfolio management systems (top right quadrant). Packages selected by Gartner for inclusion in the top quadrant provide the following features in support of project documentation:

- management of documents by versions;
- archiving;
- advanced searching within documents;
- workflow support;
- (personal) information (dashboards, views and intranet pages) tailored specifically for the receiver;
- integration of Issues, Risks and Lessons Learned Registers.

Other organisations have also researched tools for project portfolio management. A study by Dunnink et al (2005) deals with a Project Performance Improvement reference model. One of the views in this model is knowledge and document management (KDM). In this study the project and portfolio management systems of 34 suppliers are described. Document management supports the management of programme and project documents. Knowledge management is intended for the re-use of statistics gained through experience and the application of lessons learned. All PPM tools make provision for document management and are, therefore, useful for the professional and mature project management organisation (PMO).

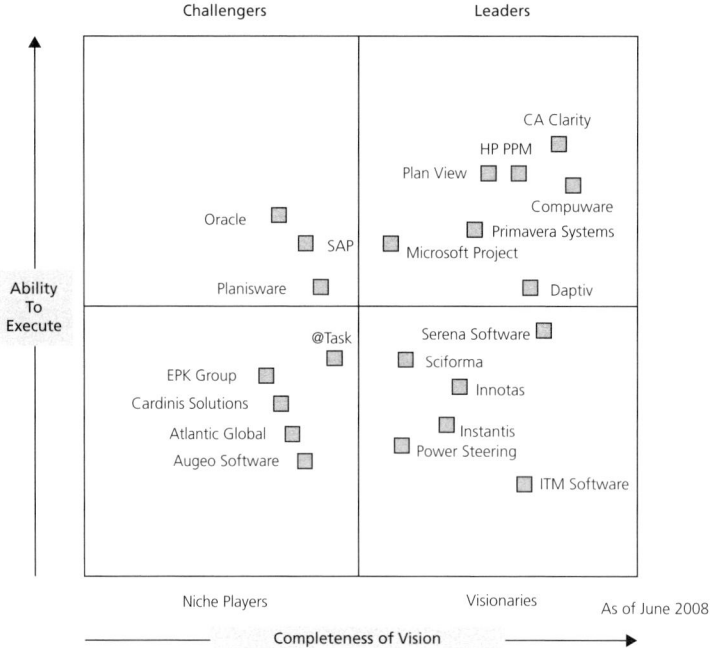

Figure 6.1   Magical quadrant for portfolio management (source Gartner 2008)

6.2   Integration of PPM tools and the document approach

The application of PPM tools can enhance the quality of information provision. It can support the organisation in achieving the next maturity level. However, the implementation of a PPM tool must not be underestimated, since it requires thorough preparation. The project management processes must be well embedded (first organise then automate). Having to record time is an important requirement. So, if the organisation is not accustomed to recording time, then a considerable change in approach should be expected with the implementation of a PPM tool.

The effects of applying PPM tools are particularly noticeable in relation to the building blocks for planning, resources, the budget and the Highlights Report. Thanks to the use of these tools, the information is more consistent. Moreover, the information is electronically available, so the project manager is required to do less manual calculation. The tools, for example, describe a product-based plan with the matching activities. Employees are linked to these activities. The employees work according to a rate and this rate is multiplied by the planned effort to determine the budget. Entering this data and the hours undertaken, together with any changes in the planning, provides the actual planning and budget utilization. The Earned Value Analysis is almost always available. The tools support the generation of logs for issues, risks and lessons learned. They also generate Checkpoint Reports (Highlights Reports and Status Reports). However, the Exceptions Report and Decisions to be taken are still lacking in these tools.

In summary the tools support operational (progress and portfolio) project management and the tactical/strategic portfolio management processes.

For static documents such as the Business Case, the PID and the End Project Report, the tool supports version management of documents and archiving. The project management process is supported by the workflow function. Online availability, filling in of compulsory documents (including reviewing and approval), e-mail notification and integrated reporting are also available.

In addition to PPM tools, groupware solutions are also becoming increasingly popular. Project team members do not all work in the same location. These groupware solutions provide, amongst other things, the opportunity for different project team members to work on the same documents in different locations, proving particularly valuable for international or virtual teams.

6.3 'SMART' templates and building blocks

The previous section explains how a PPM tool is useful for working with building blocks. However, active support of building blocks is still lacking. A new development in this area is the 'SMART' templates and electronic project management forms. The project manager registers all data only once. Think, for example, of the description of the 'why' of the project. All documents containing these building blocks will use this source information.[8] This partly addresses the drawback of having to write the same texts repeatedly. What is still lacking is the flexibility to compile a document based on existing building blocks and to add in text boxes and visual images. This is the added value of the documentation standard that I describe in this book.

One-off registration of information in the building blocks seems to support the consistency of the story-lines presented. Do 'SMART' building blocks have a future? I use the word 'seems' advisedly, for it begs the question of whether, at the start of the project, all information is already known. It is more of an iterative process, in which parallel creation of the building blocks occurs. The story-lines are an aid and a checking instrument for consistency. 'SMART' building blocks can hamper this creative process.

Intermediate forms are possible. The project owner can, for example, complete the Mandate with an electronic form. Automated checks further evaluate whether it meets the requirements of a project, or whether it relates to a maintenance task. Via the workflow of the PPM information system the Mandate subsequently arrives at the PMO.

Concrete suggestions and practical tips
- First organise, then computerise.
- Do not underestimate the implementation and deployment of a PPM aid for an organisation

---

[8] Mandate, Business Case, Project Brief and Project initiation Document

6.4 Summary

In this chapter I have described the opportunities for using supporting tools in the application of PRINCE2. In addition I have looked at knowledge and document management within project and portfolio management systems. The information systems provide consistent data for fleshing out the building blocks, such as the budget and the planning building blocks. Active support of document construction with the building block approach is (still) lacking in these tools.

In the next chapter I will outline an approach for the introduction of a documentation standard in organisations (though without using a PPM information system to achieve this).

7 From theory to practice

'A journey of a thousand miles begins with a single step'.
Mao Tse Tung

In the previous chapters you have become acquainted with the most important PRINCE2 products and the building blocks through which these products are constructed. This chapter provides handles for making these building blocks usable in your organisation. By reading this book you have taken the first step, but there is still much work to be done in the rest of your organisation. A sponsor is crucial for a project. They are also indispensable for the introduction of a documentation standard. I provide a step by step plan to help implement the documentation standard in your organisation. To do this I broadly follow the 'Solution-based working' approach of Visser et al (2005).

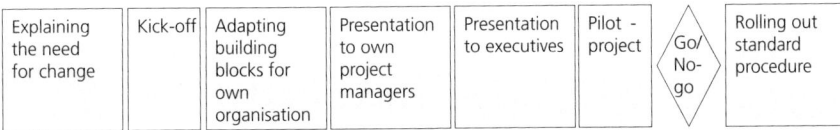

Figure 7.1 Step by step plan for implementation of documentation standard

The step by step plan can be subdivided as follows (see Figure 7.1):

1. *Explanation of the need for change:* find a sponsor at the management level within your organisation. Without a sponsor you will not succeed. Write an initial memo (in PRINCE2 terms a Project Brief) and convince/sweet-talk the sponsor. Review the projects over the past two years. Examine the documents used. Is there any standard to speak of? How were the documents received, were they read? How was the reporting on the development of the projects undertaken? The case becomes stronger if the executives were dissatisfied with the documentation previously used.

2. *Kick-off:* determine who is interested and explain the value of the (new) documentation standard. Involve potential executives and project managers. Refer to the PRINCE2 product model (Chapter 1, the fourth pair of spectacles and Chapter 2) as a starting point. Stress the disadvantage of bulky project plans and their limited use. Present the storyboard and the building block concept.

3. *Adapting building blocks for your own organisation:* define the situation that you are aspiring to. With the cooperation of enthusiastic project managers, model the building blocks according to the needs of your organisation. Use Chapter 8 as basis for this. Some building blocks are used in nearly every organisation (see Table 7.1).

No.	Building block	Changes	Explanation
B1	Documentation management	No	
B2	Mandate - <number> <project name>	No	
B3	Project background - <project name>	No	
B4	Scope - <project name>	Yes	The top half of this building block is specific. It describes the product(s) (parts) that the organisation supplies to customer groups.
B5	Business Case risk analysis - <Project name>	No	
B6	Cost benefit cash flow - <project name>	Yes	Coordinate the cost divisions with the cost structure of the financial department.
B7	Project approach - <project name>	No	
B8	Value Chain - <project name>	Yes	Describe the primary business process and the underlying part processes.
B9	Product breakdown - <project name>	No	
B10	Product breakdown work package	No	
B11	Product description - - <project name> work package	No	
B12	Resources - - <project name>	No	
B13	Planning <date> - - <project name>	No	
B14	Risks - - <project name>	No	
B15	Organisation - - <project name>	No	
B16	Budget details <date> - <project name>	No	
B17	Acceptance criteria - <project name>	Yes	Establish standard acceptance criteria
B18	Architecture and security aspects - <project name>	Yes	Discuss the architectural plan[9] and the information security plan with the IT department.
B19	Business process aspects - <project name>	Yes	Discuss the business process action plan with the department that is responsible for establishing the processes.
B20	Communication plan - <project name>	No	
B21	Quality plan - <project name>	No	
B22	Highlights Report <date> - <project name>	No	
B23	Decisions to be taken <date> - <project name>	No	
B24	Recapitulation - <project name>	No	
B25	Follow-on Action Recommendations - <project name>	No	
B26	Lessons learned - <project name>	No	
B27	Project Board actions	No	
B28	Customer satisfaction	No	
B29	Project team satisfaction	No	
B30	Issues Register	No	
B31	Risk Register	No	
B32	Lessons Learned Register	No	
B33	Action list	No	

Table 7.1 Summary of standard and corporate building blocks

[9] Refer for an explanation of these action plans to the detailed descriptions of the building blocks in Chapter 8.

4. *Presentation to project managers:* introduce the new project documentation standard to project managers. The basis for this is the presentation used for the kick-off, supplemented with the new (designed) building blocks.

5. *Presentation to executives:* familiarise the executives with the new project documentation standard. Show them the building blocks from the PID and the Status Report in particular.

6. *Pilot project (one step at a time):* select a project (with an enthusiastic executive and a project manager who feels the same). Using the building blocks, arrange for the project manager to compile a Lessons Report for the project as well as a separate Lessons Report for the documentation standard. Determine beforehand the acceptance criteria upon which decision-making will be based for the application of the new documentation standard.

7. *The go and no-go evaluation (monitoring progress):* review the Lessons Report of the documentation standard. Check the report against the specified acceptance criteria. On the basis of this testing and the review of the Lessons Report, recommend how the organisation is to proceed.

8. *Rolling out the standard procedure (determining further need for change):* implement possible changes in the standard resulting from the evaluations and the Lessons Report. Agree what the organisation should do with current projects. The Highlights Report and the Status Report are used for all projects. The End Project Report and the Lessons Report can always be developed according to the standard. Encourage the use of the new standard. For example, paste the Highlights Reports on a wall where they can be seen by the project managers. This entices them to provide their own Highlights Report the following week.

7.2 A real-life example

The IT department of a large Dutch retail business implements hundreds of changes every year. These are the result of the changing wishes of their customers, changing legislation and, of course, essential technical improvements. The biggest changes are clustered in approximately eighty projects annually. The IT department uses its own project management method. This was originally based on the method of Project Working, but since then has been modernised on the basis of PRINCE2. There are well over thirty project managers, who all work in a project management pool (PM pool).

What is important in their project management method is that a project has only one detailed realization stage. A project plan is written for this. Often a preliminary investigation is needed. It is methodically picked up in the initiation stage, of which the Project Initiation Memo (PIM) is the start point. Project managers periodically report with Checkpoint Reports. Projects are formally ended after the project evaluation.

Microsoft Word templates support the various project documents. Over the years these templates have increased in volume. This is the result of striving for comprehensiveness and accuracy. The bulky project management documentation makes no contribution to customer satisfaction.

Quite the contrary, the legibility and usefulness of the documentation does not come up to expectations.

In mid-2006, the need to drastically re-think the project approach was identified as a requirement by the management of the PM pool.

Clarifying the need for change
From interviews and discussions it is evident that project support can contribute to a greater level of satisfaction amongst customers of the IT department.

Defining the desired situation
Via the web the management of the PM pool knows the author of this book and his practical PRINCE2 approach. He is invited to present his approach during a regular PM pool session.

Determining the platform and analyzing earlier success
Following on from this, a small group of project managers is formed that examines which elements work well in the current procedure and what components of the storyboard and building block concepts could be applicable.

One step at a time
As the first step this group 'translates' the PIM into a concise decision document in PowerPoint.

Monitoring progress
With a number of new initiatives, the project managers are further asked to translate the PIM into a decision document in PowerPoint, in order to maintain contact with real practice. The group supports commitment to the essence of this approach. In addition the Project Board, which makes decisions about projects, encourages the new development.

Taking the next step
After a number of months of running trials, the PowerPoint PIM becomes the new standard. In the meantime the same process has been started for the project plan, which is more comprehensive than the PIM and has a target group. Within no time at all the first plans have been made and approved for this new way of working. The advantages of the practical PRINCE2 have come to light.

Determining further needs for change
Next the Checkpoint Report and project evaluation are addressed. The radical reorganisation results in a change of focus by the management. Although not yet quite complete, the conclusion that the practical PRINCE2 has been implemented seamlessly is accepted: the retailer has adopted the practical elements.

What are these elements?
- A plan consists of building blocks that are expanded and completed during the project;
- Keep it short and simple (KISS);

- One picture is worth a thousand words; use as many images as possible. These are sparingly supported by text;
- Following on from the above: the documentation should concentrate on the managing of the project, not on explaining or defending the solution(s).

As you can see in Figure 7.2, this retailer has taken the first steps. Currently they are investigating the extent to which the Status Report can be used as a Project Board report.

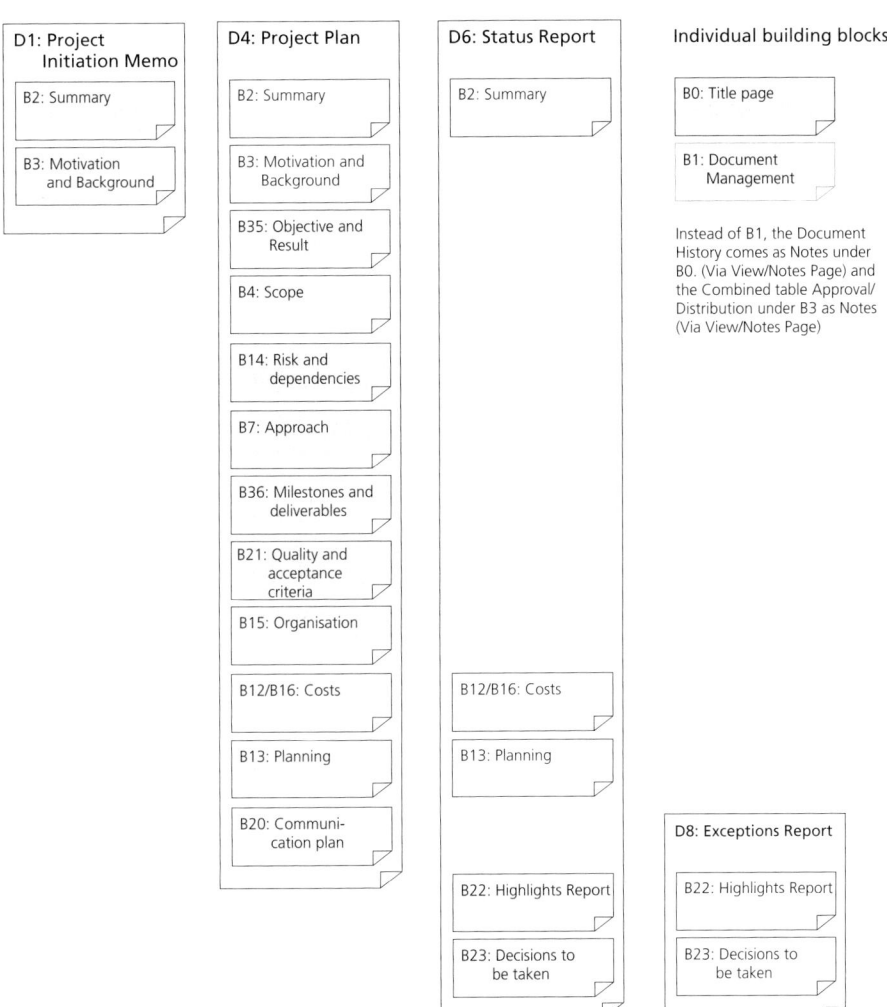

Figure 7.2 Retailer's case

8 The documentation building blocks

This chapter describes examples of the building blocks of the PRINCE2 documents. Every organisation can determine the importance of these building blocks and the information required for each building block. The organisation can also determine the building blocks it wishes to use to build its own products.

No	Sect.	Building block	Mandate	Project Brief	PID	Status Report	Highlights Report	End Project Report
B1	8.1	Document management		√	√			√
B2	8.2	Mandate - <number> <project name>	√	√	√	√		√
B3	8.3	Project background – <project name>		√	√			√
B4	8.4	Scope - <project name>		√	√			√
B5	8.5	Business Case risk analysis < project name>		√	√			√
B6	8.6	Cost benefit cash flow - <project name>		√	√			√
B7	8.7	Project approach - <project name>		√	√			
B8	8.8	Value chain - <project name>		√	√			
B9	8.9	Product breakdown – <project name>		√	√			
B10	8.10	Product breakdown - <project name> work package <name>			√			
B11	8.11	Product description - <project name> work package <name>			√			
B12	8.12	Resources - <project name>		√	√			
B13	8.13	Planning <date> - - <project name>		√	√	√		√
B14	8.14	Risks - <project name>		√	√			
B15	8.15	Organisation - <project name>			√			
B16	8.16	Budget details <date> - <project name>			√	√		√
B17	8.17	Acceptance criteria - <project name>			√			
B18	8.18	Architecture and security aspects - <project name>			√			
B19	8.19	Business process aspects – <project name>			√			
B20	8.20	Communication plan – <project name>			√			
B21	8.21	Quality plan - <project name>			√			
B22	8.22	Highlights Report <date> - <project name>				√	√	√
B23	8.23	Decisions to be taken <date> - <project name>				√		√
B24	8.24	Recapitulation - <project name>						√
B25	8.25	Follow–up action recommendations (B25) <project name>						√
B26	8.26	Lessons learned - <project name>						√
B27	8.27	Project Board actions and decisions				√		
B28	8.28	Customer satisfaction						√
B29	8.29	Project team satisfaction						√

No	Sect.	Building block	Mandate	Project Brief	PID	Status Report	Highlights Report	End Project Report
B30	8.30	Issues Register						
B31	8.31	Risk Register						
B32	8.32	Lessons Learned Register						
B33	8.33	Action list						

Table 8.1 Relationship between building blocks and PRINCE2 products

Header sheet (Title page) (B0)

	Mandate (D1)	Project Brief (D3)	PID (D4)	Status Report (D6)	Highlights Report (D5)	End Project Report (D7)
Used in		√	√	√		√

Organisations are naturally free to use a header sheet with documents. If the organisation makes use of header sheets, a minimum of the following categories should be entered in a fixed place:

- document name (for example PID or End Project Report);
- project name;
- name of project manager;
- date;
- version number.

8.1 Document Management (B1)

	Mandate (D1)	Project Brief (D3)	PID (D4)	Status Report (D6)	Highlights Report (D5)	End Project Report (D7)
Used in		✓	✓			✓

Document Management

Revision History

Version	Revision date	Status	Summary of changes	By
		Concept		
		Concept		
		Proposal		
		Approved		

Approval
This document requires approval by the following persons:
Signed approval forms are saved in the management section of the project file.

Name	Signature	Title/Position	Distribution date	Version
Sponsor				
Owner				
Sr. User				
Sr. Supplier				
PMO				

Distribution
This document is issued to:

Name	Title/Position	Distribution date	Version

This building block shows the versions of a document and the most important changes in successive versions. In 'Revision History' the 'status' field provides the opportunity to indicate the stages that the document has passed through:

- concept (under control of author);
- proposal (submitted for review);

- accepted (by project or programme manager);
- approved (see the Approval list in this building block).

The middle block provides space for the formal signing and the bottom block shows which officials have received this document – in addition to the formal signatories.

The documentation building blocks 69

8.2 Mandate - <number> <project name> (B2)

	Mandate (D1)	Project Brief (D3)	PID (D4)	Status Report (D6)	Highlights Report (D5)	End Project Report (D7)
Used in	✓	✓	✓	✓		✓

Mandate - <number> <project name>

Reasons for acting <<Filling in and replacing: Limit this document to ONE page. Current ways of working inconsistent with the market, risk [?] too high. Inadequate support from IT, market needs new products/services.>>

Objectives/benefits <<Filling in and replacing: What must be achieved, and what does the organisation yield? Costs + financial results.>>

Most important results <<Filling in and replacing: What should actually have been achieved at the end of this project?>>

Scope <<Filling in and replacing: What does/does not belong to this project that is worth mentioning?>>

Limitations <<Filling in and replacing: all limitations that you can think about: employees, budget, systems, organisation.>>

Relationship with other projects <<Filling in and replacing: projects that first have to be completed or are dependent on the results of this project.>>

Systems involved <<Filling in and replacing: names of systems known to be affected by these project results.>>

<<If known/proposal ->
Sponsor: <name>
Project Board:
<name>
<name>
<name>
<name>
Project Manager: <name>

1. Indication of budget:
2. Indication of completion time:
3. Indication of # people:
4. Type of project: << Filling in and replacing: protecting running of business, contractual obligations, laws and regulations, improvements.>>
Revision: <number>, <date>
Project may start: Yes/No

This building block is the foundation of all PRINCE2 documents. The building block describes the 'why' (reasons to act), the 'what' (objectives/benefits) and the 'how' of the project (most important results). In addition, this building block shows the context of the project. It describes the scope, the limitations, the relationships with other projects and the systems involved. Finally, this building block also indicates the members of the Project Board (as soon as they are known, thus included in the PID anyway) and the size of the project (budget, completion period and number of people).

8.3 Project background - <project name> (B3)

	Mandate (D1)	Project Brief (D3)	PID (D4)	Status Report (D6)	Highlights Report (D5)	End Project Report (D7)
Used in		✓	✓			✓

Project Background - <project name>

Context of project
<<why is it needed, what is the preceding history, how does it fit into the programme?>>

The Project background describes the context of the project. Examples of this are:

- the development and introduction of a new product;
- a legislative change by government;
- a compulsory directive from formal supervisors;
- improvement of a process in which interruptions or mistakes occur.

8.4 Scope - <project name> (B4)

	Mandate (D1)	Project Brief (D3)	PID (D4)	Status Report (D6)	Highlights Report (D5)	End Project Report (D7)
Used in		✓	✓			✓

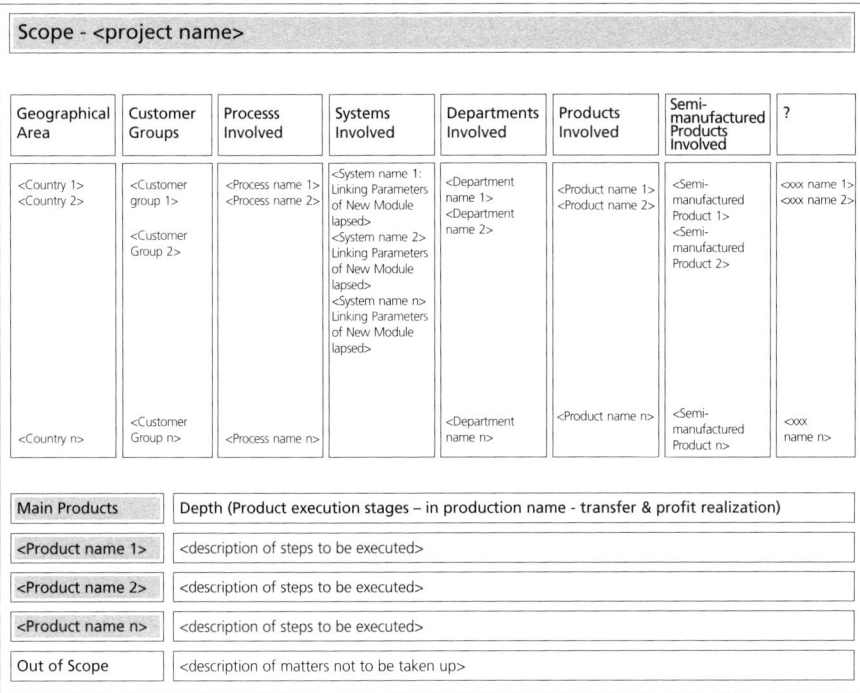

The top part of this building block indicates a number of characteristics of the organisation. Are there any different geographical areas, different customer groups, types of products or semi-manufactured products? In the financial world there are different portfolios and different financial instruments. All the processes, departments and systems that are involved complete the Scope. In addition, the Scope building block describes the depth of each product in terms of the number of product execution stages. Finally, matters are included where it is unclear as to whether they belong to the project. An explicit statement in the Out of Scope box makes it clear that the project will not deliver these products.

8.5 Business Case risk analysis - <project name> (B5)

	Mandate (D1)	Project Brief (D3)	PID (D4)	Status Report (D6)	Highlights Report (D5)	End Project Report (D7)
Used in		✓	✓			✓

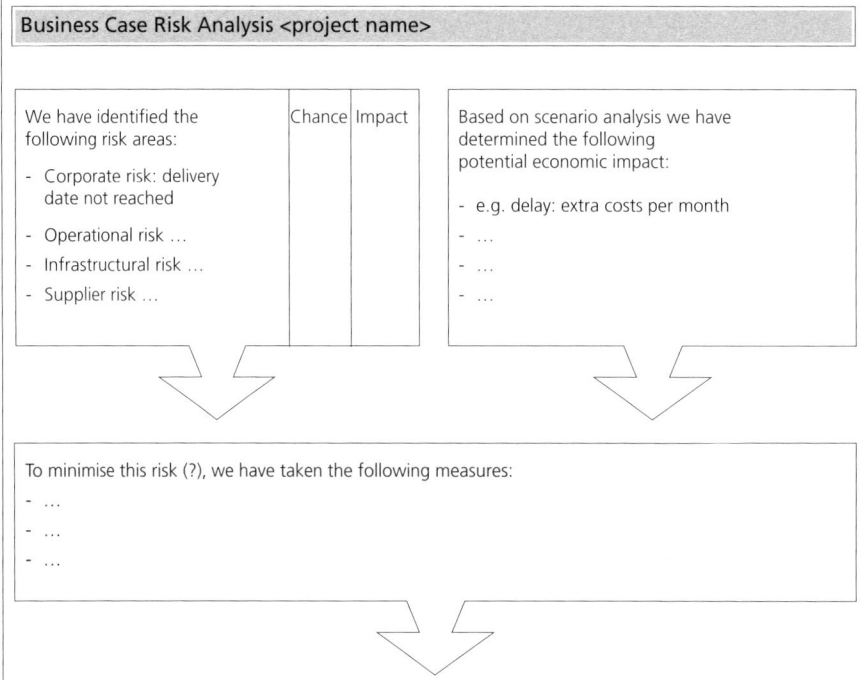

These building blocks specify the risk areas. The building block further provides an analysis of the impact of the risks on the Business Case. This is undertaken in relation to the Net Present Value (NPV), Internal Rate of Return (IRR) or the payback period. In the following section covering the Cost Benefit Cash Flow (B6) building block, I clarify these terms. In addition this building block indicates the measures that should be taken to minimise the risks. Also refer to the Risks (B14) building block for a summary of measures to control risks.

8.6 Cost benefit cash flow - <project name> (B6)

	Mandate (D1)	Project Brief (D3)	PID (D4)	Status Report (D6)	Highlights Report (D5)	End Project Report (D7)
Used in		✓	✓			✓

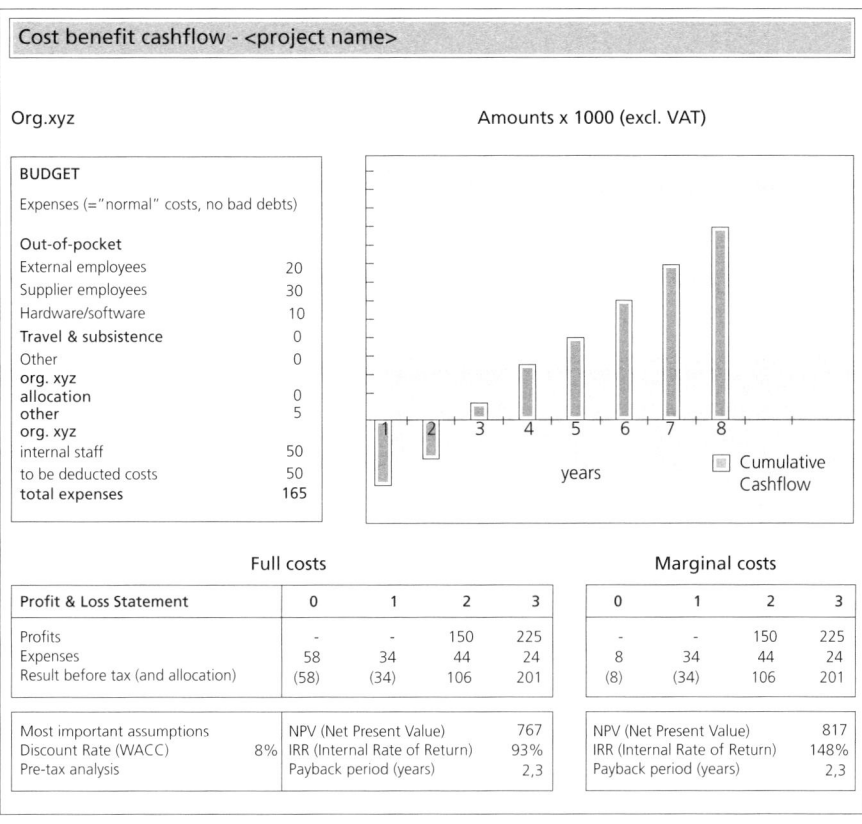

This building block calculates the cash flow of the project, the Net Present Value (NPV) and the Internal Rate of Return (IRR). The building block further indicates the basis of the costs, the benefits and the payback period. The outcomes of the calculations are based on this building block. The underlying detailed calculations must be available, but they are not a part of the PID.

The following concepts are used in this building block:

The Present Value (PV)
The Present Value (PV) of an amount, X euro, over a time period of N years and at rate of interest P, is the amount X that is yielded at compound interest with the stated interest rate after a

period of N years. If you receive an amount of 100 euro over one year and the inflation amounts to 4% for that year, you will be able to buy less for the 100 euro over a year than you currently can. At this moment 100 euro can be compared (in terms of purchasing power) with 104 euro in a year's time. A 100 euro in a year's time can be compared with 96,15 euro at present. The NP of 100 euro is 96,15 euro. One can say that 96,15 euro equals '100 euro in 1 year's time' in cash.

Stated as a formula:

$$PV = x * \left(\frac{1}{1 + \frac{P}{100}}\right)^N$$

$$100 * \left(\frac{1}{1,04}\right)^1 = 96,15$$

Net Present Value (NPV)
You can calculate Present Values in the same way. In this way you can compare the effects of expenditures and incomes occurring at different times. The Present Value of costs deducted from the Present Value of benefits provides the so-called Net Present Value of a project. Example: You invest 100 euro now and in a year's time you invest a further 50 euro. In 2 years time you receive 100 euro and in 3 years 100 euro again. The interest amounts to 4%. The Present Value of the investment is at present: 100 + 48,08 = 148,08 euro. The Present Value of the benefits is: 100 (over two years) = 92,46 100 (over 3 years) = 88,90. Total NP = 181,36. The Net Present Value is 181,36 – 148,08 = 33,28 euro.

Internal Rate of Return (IRR)
The Internal Rate of Return of a project is a benchmark of the acceptability of an investment for the executive. If you suppose that the Net Present Value is nil, you can calculate the Internal Rate of Return. With a choice between two or more projects, the project with the highest Internal Rate of Return should be given preference. In addition the Internal Rate of Return must be higher than the yield, should the money be invested.

Payback Period
The Payback Period is the period in which the benefits equal the costs of the project. With the application of the Payback Period as the criterion for project selection in the PPM process, the management selects the project which has the shortest payback period.

WACC
The WACC (*Weighted Average Cost of Capital*) is the weighted average cost of the weighted wealth of a business. Managers, who are looking for expansion opportunities or take-overs, often use the WACC. With this managers can calculate the costs that the business incurs over the lifetime of the assets for which the business is financed. The WACC distinguishes between Foreign and Own Assets. The WACC is calculated by multiplying the costs per asset type (Own and Foreign) with the rate of the total assets. The financial department can furnish the WACC. The manner of calculating the WACC lies outside the scope of this book.

8.7 Project approach - <project name> (B7)

	Mandate (D1)	Project Brief (D3)	PID (D4)	Status Report (D6)	Highlights Report (D5)	End Project Report (D7)
Used in		✓	✓			

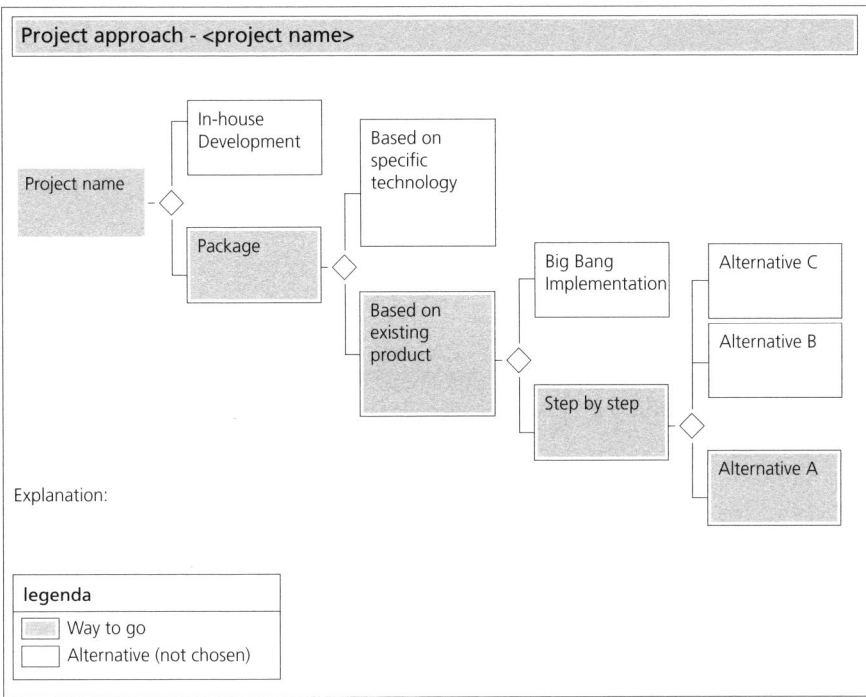

This building block illustrates the project steps and the decisions that are taken in respect of the approach. Along with the decisions taken, the corresponding 'road not taken' is also described. This review can be used to determine to what extent the project manager meets the expectations of the executive and other stakeholders. Test the opinions in the organisation concerning the project approach in due time.

When selecting the approach, take account of the following points:

- if available, use a standard approach for similar projects;
- choose the approach with the fewest risks and uncertainties;
- for risky projects, examine alternative scenarios.

The approach is not just a list of activities to be executed. The approach shows which decisions have been taken and which road has been chosen. For example, you have the choice between buying things ready-made or making what you need yourself. The approach describes the choice and the arguments for it.

If the approach is initially not sufficiently clear, then running a workshop with the stakeholders can help to clarify matters. Creativity is important. It is a good thing to define a number of game rules before the workshop.

The game rules for creative thinking are:

- keeping an open mind (open focus);
- frankness within the group, reticence outside the group;
- extra attention to naïve ideas (break through presuppositions);
- reinforcing ideas ('Yes, good and…').

Evaluating ideas can be done by means of the framework below.

	Known ideas	New ideas
Not (yet)		Dreaming the future
Workable	Existing ideas	Innovations

For the process of creative thinking you can use the following steps.

1. Describe the project as you see it now: 'What is a…?'
2. Describe the parts comprising the project result: 'What are the parts of a …?'
3. Describe for each part what the project result would look like without that part. Let your imagination go. Take the game rules for creative thinking into account: 'What, if… not …?'
4. Position the proposed ideas for each part in the framework to evaluate the workability of the ideas. With innovative ideas, describe the risks in the risk building block (B14).
5. Translate the ideas into possible steps in the project. Determine which ideas or roads within the project you wish to reject. These rejected ideas come to light in the project approach as the alternatives not chosen ('the road not taken').

The laying out of a garden
You want to lay out a garden. Which parts (Product breakdown) do you identify: terrace, borders, pond, fencing, etc. Are you going to dig a pond or purchase a ready-made one (existing idea)? Is the pond to be placed in the ground (existing idea)? Suppose you do not want to dig a pond, is there an alternative? Yes, for example above the ground (innovation). Are you designing the garden yourself or are you having a design done; are you doing the digging yourself or are you having the digging done for you? Ditto for the building of the terrace. What sequence are you going to follow? The approach can then be: garden designed by third party (alternative of designing it yourself is rejected because of a lack of knowledge/insight). Next dig pond myself and build terrace. The alternative of having the terrace built is rejected because of high costs.

8.8 Value Chain - <project name> (B8)

	Mandate (D1)	Project Brief (D3)	PID (D4)	Status Report (D6)	Highlights Report (D5)	End Project Report (D7)
Used in		✓	✓			

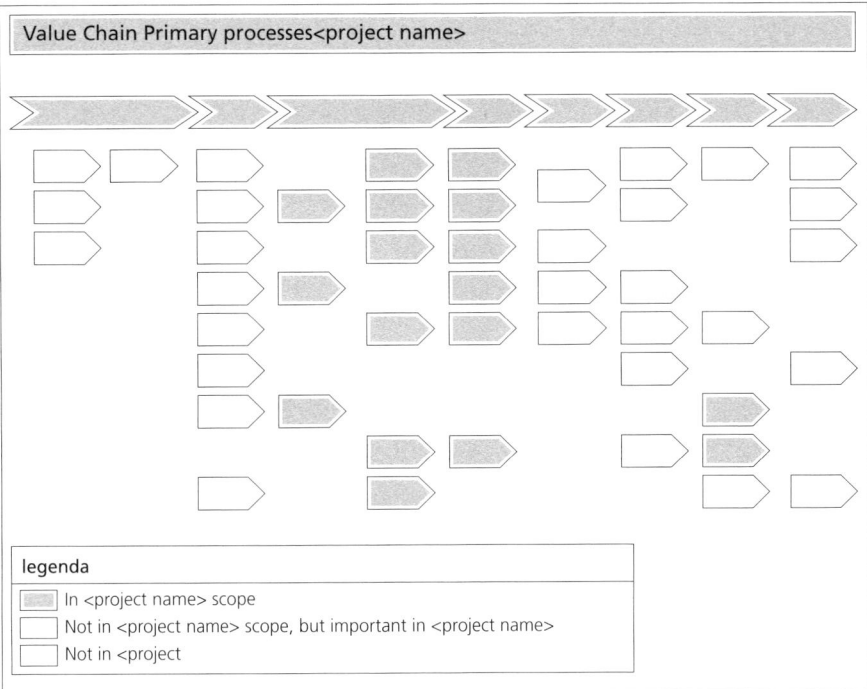

This building block describes the value chain of the organisation. In this building block all business processes that impact upon the project are stated. In addition, other business processes are named that are important, but that do not impact upon the project (they are probably relevant for the Acceptance test). Every organisation has a value chain. As a starting point for the description, generic models are sometimes available from consultants and branch organisations. These models can be developed for your organisation. Insight into the processes that change the project makes it possible to coordinate with other projects that are adapting the same process at the same time.

8.9 Product Breakdown

	Mandate (D1)	Project Brief (D3)	PID (D4)	Status Report (D6)	Highlights Report (D5)	End Project Report (D7)
Used in		✓	✓			

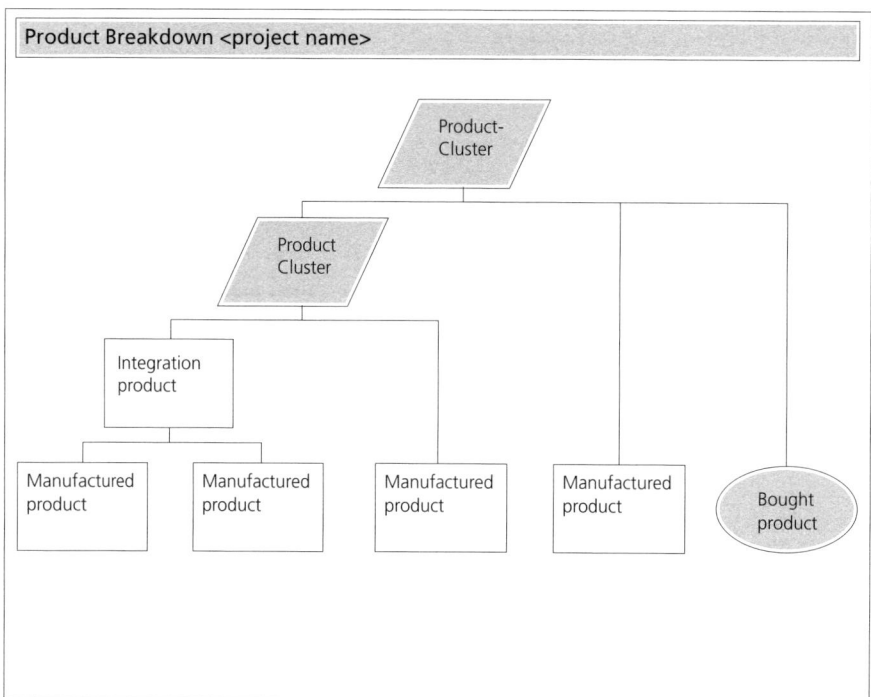

PRINCE2 uses product-based planning as its point of departure. The basis for this is the Product breakdown. This breakdown describes the relationship between the most important intermediary and end products of the project. On the basis of this breakdown, the project manager is able to undertake the planning for the delivery of (intermediary) products. The structure is also the basis for dividing the project into product parts (per product cluster). The breakdown is also useful for the development of the work packages (per product).

A breakdown can be done in different ways. The choice depends on the project and the project manager. Choose different points of view to describe structures, so that you get a total overview of the products. A breakdown of a garden can be based on trees, shrubs, plants, grass, etc. The breakdown can also be based on space for lying down, space for walking, storage space, etc. The division must be simple to explain and should not raise any new questions.

The question of how deep the breakdown should go is not easy to answer. Do not go any further with the detail than is necessary for the successful running of the project. This prevents unnecessary effort with the plans (that subsequently would only remain unused). Stop doing the breakdown if the executive has no interest in the delivery of intermediary products - unless you need the breakdown for the purposes of project management and quality checks.

8.10 Product breakdown - <project name> Work package - <work package name> (B10)

	Mandate (D1)	Project Brief (D3)	PID (D4)	Status Report (D6)	Highlights Report (D5)	End Project Report (D7)
Used in			✓			

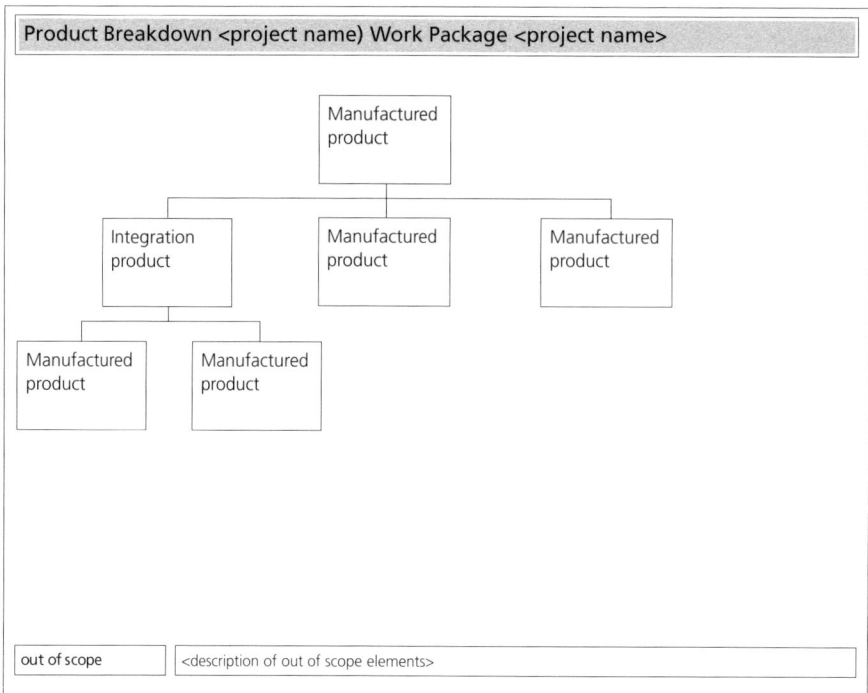

This building block is a further development of the product parts in work packages (D5). The building block shows the relationship between the products or product parts. The starting points for the product breakdown at a project level also apply to the work package. To prevent misunderstandings, this building block also describes what does not belong to the work package. This happens in a similar manner to that used for the Scope Building Block (B4).

8.11 Product description - <project name> <name> (B11)

	Mandate (D1)	Project Brief (D3)	PID (D4)	Status Report (D6)	Highlights Report (D5)	End Project Report (D7)
Used in			✓			

Product Description <project name> Work Package <name>

<product name>	<description and purpose of the product>

Reviewed by:	Quality criteria	Quality method
<quality criterion 1> <quality criterion 2> <quality criterion n>	<describe how the criteria are to be controlled>	<name 1> <name 2> <name n>

Lay-out, format: <<Complete and replace: description of the lay-out, format, with particular reference to existing standards and documents>>

Techniques, Processes and Procedures used: <<Complete and replace: activities or products that must first be completed or the interdependence with other work packages>>

Contacts: <<Complete and replace: contact names>>

Delivery requirements: <<Complete and replace: e.g. deadlines, etc.>>

Additional requirements/agreements: <<Complete and replace:>>

The Product Description describes the product (part), including the quality criteria, the quality method and the reviewer of the quality criteria. In addition, the building block specifies the techniques, processes and procedures, delivery requirements (suppliers/contacts, additional requirements/agreements) and relationships with other activities or products or product parts.

Within a Work Package (D5) there can be different Product Descriptions. A work package for a telephone, for example, consists of a Product Description of the telephone handset, a Product Description of the network adapter and a Product Description of the telephone cradle.

8.12 Resources - <project name> (B12)

	Mandate (D1)	Project Brief (D3)	PID (D4)	Status Report (D6)	Highlights Report (D5)	End Project Report (D7)
Used in		✓	✓			

Resources Budget <project name>

Product name	Task	Dept	Name	Indication days/week	From	To

The Resources Building Block provides a general indication of the type of employees (position) required, the level of required effort and a rough time frame for the availability of these employees. It makes no sense to start a project if the resources (internal or external) are not available. For the PID (D4) these building blocks are worked out in detail. It is not sufficient to simply list any employee without being specific and permission is needed to free up the desired employees who have been nominated for the project.

8.13 Planning <date> - <project name> (B13)

	Mandate (D1)	Project Brief (D3)	PID (D4)	Status Report (D6)	Highlights Report (D5)	End Project Report (D7)
Used in		✓	✓	✓		✓

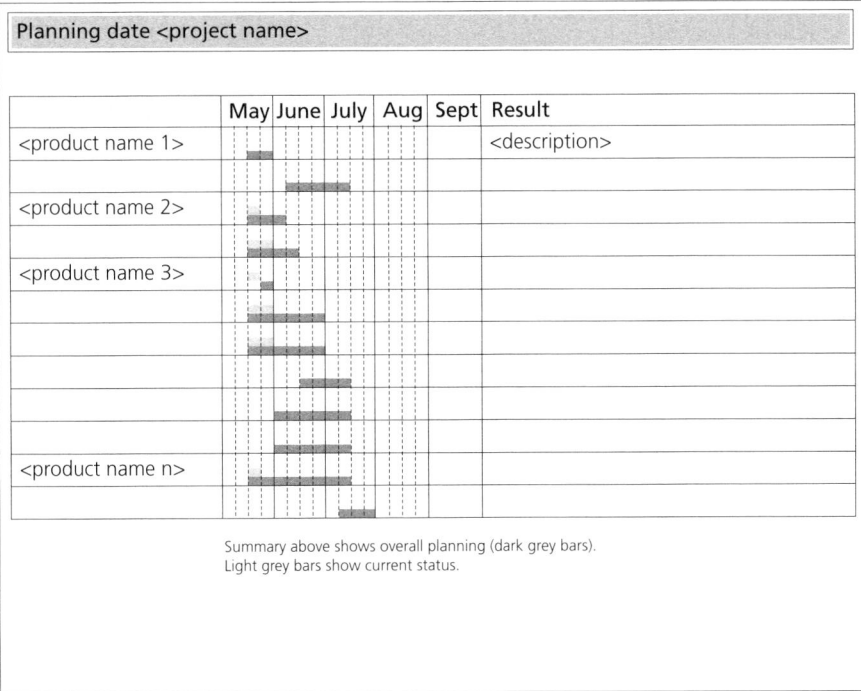

This building block provides an image of the planning of the project for those involved. The Planning must be legible to the Project Board members. A good plan is based on the products (see building blocks B9, B10 and B11). Very often an outline plan suffices. The project manager can work with a detailed plan, but this is not as relevant for the Project Board. If you use MS Project© as a planning tool, you can take a snapshot (small photographic icon) and include the 'photo' in this building block.

8.14 Risks - <project name> (B14)

	Mandate (D1)	Project Brief (D3)	PID (D4)	Status Report (D6)	Highlights Report (D5)	End Project Report (D7)
Used in		✓	✓			

Risks <project name>

No.	Event (Description)	Result	Effect	Chance	Impact	Action/Measure	Responsible (in Project Board)
1							
2							
3				4	3	prevention	
4						reduction	
5						acceptance	
						contingency plan	
						transfer	

Legend
Chance: 0 to 4 (impossible, low, average, high, definitely)
Impact: 0 to 4 (imperceptible, low, rather serious, very serious, catastrophic)

This building block forms the basis of the Risk Register. The first version is developed as part of the Risk Analysis in the Project Brief. The building block is completed and updated. This is the translation of the risks that are identified in the Business Case. The description of risks is done in terms of:

- a possible event;
- the likely result of an event;
- the effect of the project in terms of the budget, completion time and quality.

In addition to this description, the possibility of action and the impact of a risk are also described. Finally, the required measures are recorded (in terms of actions, additional budget or resources).

It is important to mention in the PID who has the final responsibility on behalf of the Project Board for the risk measures. You can nominate different actions and follow-on actions, but risks cannot be excluded. It is therefore important to indicate beforehand how to react in the event of an (unexpected) risk occurring.

8.15 Organisation (B15)

	Mandate (D1)	Project Brief (D3)	PID (D4)	Status Report (D6)	Highlights Report (D5)	End Project Report (D7)
Used in			✓			

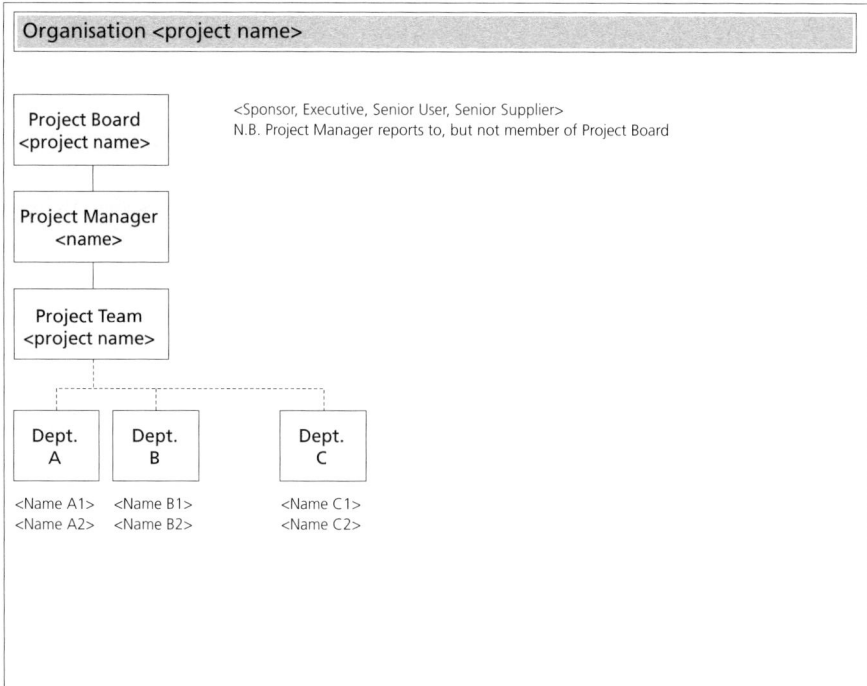

This building block describes the structure of the project. The executive, the senior user and the senior supplier are represented in the Project Board. Tasks, authority and responsibilities should be clearly described. It should explicitly state who the project manager is (reports to the Project Board, but is not a member) and which employees are part of the project. Ensure that when the team is put together, the individual qualities of the employees are known. The success of the project starts with the success of the team members. An aid to putting the team together is the team roles identified by Belbin (2006). Belbin researched the circumstances that influence team collaboration. How can it be that teams with talented individuals fail, while teams consisting of modest talents are successful? In addition to clear objectives, open communication and a realization of responsibility, a balanced distribution of team roles is necessary for a successful project team. Belbin distinguished the following roles:

1. Chairman: relatively dominant and strongly oriented towards achieving objectives.
2. Shaper: opportunistic, realistic and rather emotional, but also determined and fearless.

3. Plant: somewhat introverted, serious and creative, and sometimes has unexpectedly great ideas.
4. Monitor/evaluator: thinks of different possibilities, while the other roles are often focused on just one alternative.
5. Implementer: is conservative, conscientious and uses their common sense. They can organise, work hard and are practical.
6. Resource investigator: is enthusiastic and a true networker, poses the correct questions at the correct moment to the correct people.
7. Teamworker: strongly focused on their environment with a friendly, sensitive personality and with an interest in people.
8. Completer/finisher: is orderly, painstaking, somewhat of a perfectionist and completes matters.

8.16 Budget details <date> - <project name> (B16)

	Mandate (D1)	Project Brief (D3)	PID (D4)	Status Report (D6)	Highlights Report (D5)	End Project Report (D7)
Used in		✓	✓			✓

Budget Details <date> <project name>

Item x 1000 euro	This period	Total to date	Forecast	Budget	Budget surplus	Still to go
External employees	5	10	25	30	20	15
Outsourcer	3	8	21	20	12	13
Hardware/software	5	10	22	20	10	12
Training & subsistence costs	0	5	5	5	0	0
Other	5	5	7	5	0	2
Out-of-pocket total	18	38	80	80	42	42
Internal employees	5	10	13	10	0	3
Other	5	10	18	20	10	8
Total	28	58	111	110	52	53

This building block forms the basis for reporting on the utilization of the budget. It provides the essential budget for the project in the PID. This budget is subdivided into (out-of-pocket) costs to be paid to third parties and internal costs. Costs to be paid to third parties are subdivided into:

- external employees;
- hardware and software;
- training, travel and subsistence costs;
- other.

The project manager reports about the running costs according to the following categories:

- costs incurred during the reporting period;
- total costs to date;

- costs still to be incurred up until the time of delivery;
- approved budget.

On the basis of these categories the following sections are derived:

- budget still available (to be compared with costs still to be incurred);
- forecast of total costs at the time of delivery (total costs to date and costs still to be incurred up until the time of delivery).

Through the use of these categories Project Board members can gain insight into the financial health of the project.

In addition to the procedure outlined earlier, you can make use of the Earned Value Analysis (EVA). For examples of this refer to Kerzner (2003) or Portny (2004). The EVA is a method by which the value of the work done is compared with the value of the work that should have been done. For this you multiply the hours estimated to complete a job on a fixed date with the corresponding rate (that has been used to determine the budget). It is not necessary to know how much has actually been spent. For the EVA only the amount of work fully completed and the corresponding value of that work are relevant. You can perform the EVA for separate tasks, groups of tasks and for all tasks in the project.

This approach has a number of advantages:

- it is only necessary to measure the amount of completed work in respect of the total of the work still to be done;
- the measuring is often simple to put into practice, as long as the unit of the work is the same (this could be money, but also the number of bricks delivered, bicycles, etc.);
- the measuring is quick to do, the total cost is simple to calculate on the basis of the total number of units X the cost per unit.

Measuring and calculating these particulars provide the opportunity of reporting on the status of the project. An insight into trends is also gained. Furthermore, the organisation builds up a historical database that can be used by project managers in the future. In the EVA the following terms and ratios are relevant:

- (BCWS) Budgeted Cost of Work Scheduled;
- (BCWP) Budgeted Cost for Work Performed;
- (ACWP) Actual Cost for Work Performed;
- (SVAR or SV) Schedule Variance = (BCWP -/- BCWS);
- (CVAR or CV) Cost Variance = (BCWP -/- ACWP);
- (EAC) Estimated Cost At Completion;
- (BAC) Budget At Completion;
- (EVAC) Estimated Variance At Completion.

A negative Schedule Variance (SV) means that the project is lagging behind in terms of budget utilization. A negative Cost Variance (CV) means that the project is lagging behind in terms of planning and has a budget overrun.

8.17 Acceptance criteria - <project name> (B17)

	Mandate (D1)	Project Brief (D3)	PID (D4)	Status Report (D6)	Highlights Report (D5)	End Project Report (D7)
Used in			✓			✓

Acceptance Criteria <project name>

All products delivered comply with the quality criteria and have been seen and approved (see Quality building block).

How is Quality Control done if the project manager is not technically qualified? …

Change Management and Quality Control methods are in line with the size and complexity of the project.

Prepared by the supplier and checked by the client. Is this quality criterion adequate? …

Supplemental acceptance criteria formulated by executive? ……

This building block summarizes all the acceptance criteria. This provides the foundation for the eventual closure of the project. The project manager knows the criteria in terms of how the executive will review the project at the end. The criteria furthermore provide protection to the project manager against unapproved claims.

8.18 Architectural and security aspects <project name> (B18)

	Mandate (D1)	Project Brief (D3)	PID (D4)	Status Report (D6)	Highlights Report (D5)	End Project Report (D7)
Used in			✓			

Architecture and Information Security Aspects <project name>

Architectural products: Architecture Action Plan (Example plan and activities)

Action*	Description/ Reasons	Delivery Date	Executed by:
Test proposed solution with the planned architecture	Ensure that the valid architecture principles and basic principles have been addressed.		Project and Arch. Team
	Approved by Architecture authority		Yes/No

Information Security products: IP Action Plan (Example plan and activities)

Action	Description/ Reasons	Delivery Date	Executed by:
Execute risk analysis	Determine threats, control measures and impact on the business to provide a basis for insight into the corresponding risks.		Project team and ISO**
Approve Disaster Recovery Plan	Delivery of measures enabling re-adjustment of infrastructure in the event of a disaster.		Project team and ISO
Approve external link	External link with (for example) an external data provider must be certified before the link can be used.		Project team and ISO
Delivery of security settings and parameters document	All IT infrastructure components must be designed in accordance with the security requirements. This is indicated in the security settings and parameters document.		Project team and ISO
Delivery of authorisation matrix	An accurate authorisation matrix is essential to prevent unauthorised use.		Project team and ISO
	Approved by ISO		Yes/No

* The actions indicated are examples. They are not necessarily an aspect of the action plans but do occur often.
** ISO: Information Security Officer

This building block is the result of a consultation between architecture and information experts. Architecture experts are responsible for the design of the technical infrastructure and the information systems (including links between these systems). The architecture experts test whether the proposed project solutions fit in with the future vision of the organisation (*the planned architecture*). Information security officers are responsible, amongst other things, for undertaking risk analyses (determining threatening situations and the appropriate control measures), setting up a disaster recovery plan and keeping the authorisation matrix updated (who is responsible for performing which specific duty). In this building block all project activities are indicated that relate to the computer architecture and information security. In consultation with the relevant officials, the project manager comes to agreements concerning the architecture and information security documents, such as an Architectural plan, a Risk analysis, a Contingency plan, etc.

8.19 Business process aspects - <project name> (B19)

	Mandate (D1)	Project Brief (D3)	PID (D4)	Status Report (D6)	Highlights Report (D5)	End Project Report (D7)
Used in			✓			

Business Process Aspects <project name>

BPR products: Business Process Action Plan (Example plan and activities)

Action	Description/ Reasons	Delivery date	By
Design	Define the corporate processes.		Project team
	Define the organisational units.		Project team
	Define the number of new processes (norm 24 hours/process).		Project team/ BPR
	Define the number of existing processes (norm 16 hours/process).		Project team/ BPR
	Define the essential BPR capacity.		Project team/ BPR
	Define the period in which activities have to be performed.		Project team/ BPR
	Provide process descriptions based on the defined processes		BPR
Implementation	Define the change period for the new process architecture.		BPR
	All processes need to be approved by the process owner.		BPR/ Business
Archiving	Record the processes in the corporate tool (norm 2 hours/process).		BPR
Delivery and work instructions	The work instructions, based on the new or adapted processes are the responsibility of the line management.		Business
		Approved by BPR*	Yes/No

* BPR Business Process Redesign team

In this building block those involved are provided with an overview of all activities for the purpose of adapting the business processes. Think, for instance, of process redesigning that might arise as a result of external requirements (Sarbanes-Oxley, SAS70 declaration, or regulators such as the Financial Markets Authority (FMA), the Nederlandsche Bank (DNB), or specific legislative changes).

8.20 Communication plan - <project name> (B20)

	Mandate (D1)	Project Brief (D3)	PID (D4)	Status Report (D6)	Highlights Report (D5)	End Project Report (D7)
Used in			✓			

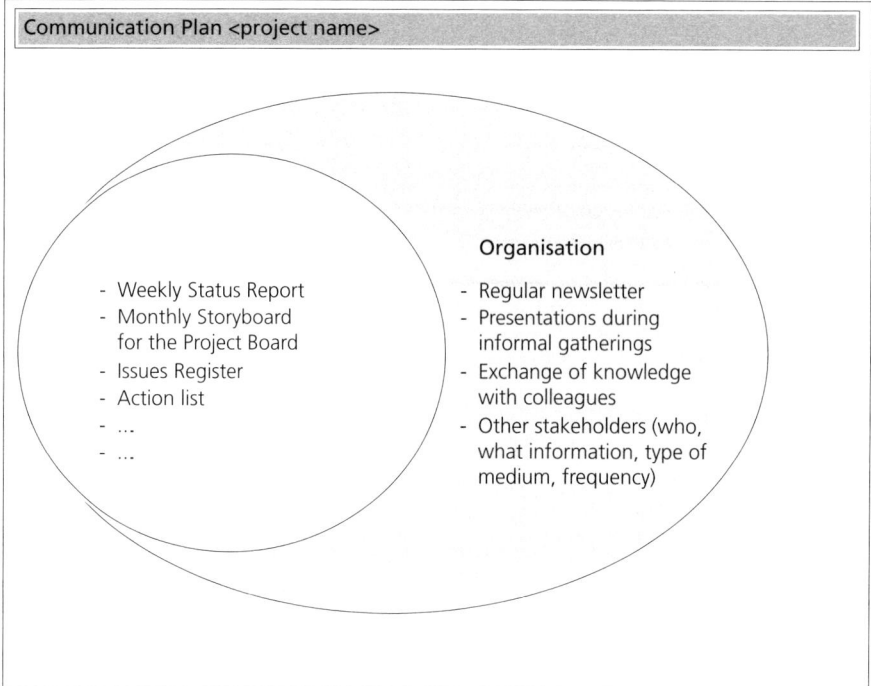

The Communication plan describes the objective, the message, the planning, the means and those responsible for project communication. In terms of project communication, think of news reports on the corporate intranet, presentation sessions and formal reports for the benefit of the Project Board and the sponsors. You can record the information in a table.

Objective	Message	Planning	Means	By whom	Target group
			News report		Project team
			Intranet		Project Board
					Sponsors

For the purpose of the Communication plan an analysis of those involved (stakeholder analysis) is useful. Establish their interest in the results of the project. Ask yourself what information stakeholders need and how often they would wish to receive such information.

8.21 Quality plan - <project name> (B21)

	Mandate (D1)	Project Brief (D3)	PID (D4)	Status Report (D6)	Highlights Report (D5)	End Project Report (D7)
Used in			✓			

Quality Plan <project name>		
Product	Quality Criteria	To be reviewed by:
<Product name 1>	<Quality Criterion 1> <Quality Criterion 2> <Quality Criterion n>	<name 1> <name 2> <name n>
<Product name n>	<Quality Criterion 1> <Quality Criterion 2> <Quality Criterion n>	<name 1> <name 2> <name n>

This building block describes the quality criteria for each product. It indicates, for each criterion, who will be responsible for reviewing it according to the PRINCE2 theme Quality (Th6). All products must be indicated in the Scope Building Block (B4).

8.22 Highlights Report <date> - <project name> (B22)

	Mandate (D1)	Project Brief (D3)	PID (D4)	Status Report (D6)	Highlights Report (D5)	End Project Report (D7)
Used in				✓	✓	✓

Highlights Report <date> <project name>

Objectives:
-
-
-

Initial delivery date: dd/mm/yy

	RAG Status
Planning	Amber
Resources	Amber
Issues	Amber
Costs	Green
Scope	Red

Most important products, results	Delivery date	New delivery date	Indicator	% Complete	Needed for completion
1 <Product name 1>	dd/mm/yy	dd/mm/yy	Green	Xx	X man-days
2 <Product name 1>	dd/mm/yy	dd/mm/yy	Amber	Xx	X man-days
n <Product name 1>	dd/mm/yy	dd/mm/yy	Complete	100	

	Issue	Consequences	Measures
1		In terms of: planning, budget, resources and implications for other projects	
2			
3			

Name of Project Manager, telephone number

The Highlights Report describes the most important products of the project. A product traffic light is specified for every product (item). This product traffic light indicates how the production of the product compares with the planning. The Highlights Report also describes a number of project traffic lights (top, right on the Highlights Report) in respect of planning, resources, issues, costs and the scope. In consultation with the executive it is possible to extend the traffic lights. If a traffic light is on amber or red, then there must be an issue that explains why this is the case. In addition to the description, the Highlights Report indicates the likely consequences of this issue for the project and the measures that have already been taken.

To determine the Resources traffic light, the following questions can be asked:

- Are all the necessary people available for the planned activity?
- Are the assigned persons sufficiently equipped to undertake the planned activities (in terms of expertise, skills and motivation)?
- Is there adequate cooperation within the team?
- Have the preconditions for executing the activities been fulfilled (for example: is the necessary information available)?
- Do the employees take an active part in the project meetings and other project activities?

If three or more questions have 'yes' responses, the traffic light is green. With one or no positive response the traffic light is red. With two positive responses the traffic light is amber.

8.23 Decisions to be taken <date> - <project name> (B23)

	Mandate (D1)	Project Brief (D3)	PID (D4)	Status Report (D6)	Highlights Report (D5)	End Project Report (D7)
Used in				✓	✓	✓

Decisions to be made <date> <project name>

Explanation of issue <n>, Requested decision <m>
- Alternative 1
  - Consequences for project (time, costs, resources, scope)
- Alternative 2
  - Consequences for project (time, costs, resources, scope). Preferred alternative of project team:
- Alternative preferred by project team: …

Explanation of issue <p>, Requested decision <q>
- Alternative 1
  - Consequences for project (time, costs, resources, scope)
- Alternative 2
  - Consequences for project (time, costs, resources, scope). Preferred alternative of project team:
- Alternative preferred by project team: …

The final building block in the Status Report is Decisions to be taken. If the project runs according to expectations, then in principle there are no decisions to be taken. In this situation it is not necessary for the Project Board to meet (the 'Management by Exception' principle of PRINCE2). If there is a decision that is required, it should be stipulated what the consequences are in terms of costs, planning and resources. Depending on the number of decisions, this building block can occur several times in the Status Report.

8.24 Recapitulation - <Project name> (B24)

	Mandate (D1)	Project Brief (D3)	PID (D4)	Status Report (D6)	Highlights Report (D5)	End Project Report (D7)
Used in						✓

Recapitulation <Project name>

Most important products to be delivered	Delivered products		Project team
- .... -	- ... -.		- .... (PM) - .... -

Most important reasons for exceeding costs/time	Scope-changes		
- .... -	#	Budget	☐ Original budget ■ Budget-overrun
		Time	☐ Original completion period (wks) ■ Completion period overrun

The recapitulation describes the intended and completed products. In addition, this building block provides a summary of the most important project employees (who could perhaps be used again should a similar project present itself). Finally, this building block shows the quality of the original planning and the budget against the completion time, as well as the costs incurred (including the reasons for any change).

8.25 Follow-on Action Recommendations - <project name> (B25)

	Mandate (D1)	Project Brief (D3)	PID (D4)	Status Report (D6)	Highlights Report (D5)	End Project Report (D7)
Used in						✓

Follow-on action recommendations <project name>

Action	Description/Reasons	Delivery date	Operative
Resolving Project issue 1		dd/mm/yy	
Resolving Project issue 2			
Reduce Risk 1			
Reduce Risk 2			
Recommendation 1			
Recommendation n			
Post-project Review Plan	State who has to record the benefits from the business case (including how and when)		PM, Stakeholders, PMO department
Post-project Review Plan meeting	Participants and date of the Post-project Review Plan meeting		PM, PMO department,

This building block describes all outstanding issues, risks and recommendations that the organisation still has to address. For every follow-on action it is indicated who the responsible person is and what the end date for this action is. The 'post project review' is also indicated as an action point (operative, planning, persons involved) to ensure that the organisation reviews the extent to which the benefits have been realized.

This action list makes it possible to end a project and to transfer all follow-on actions to nominated employees. In this way the project manager can be released from their assignment. Pending actions are covered and safe-guarded in the line organisation.

8.26 Lessons Report - <project name> (B26)

	Mandate (D1)	Project Brief (D3)	PID (D4)	Status Report (D6)	Highlights Report (D5)	End Project Report (D7)
Used in						✓

The Lessons Report is a building block in the End Project Report. For a comprehensive report the project manager uses an independent Lessons Report (D12). Based on the strong and weak points in the project, lessons can be established for future projects.

To help compile this report the following questions may help you:

- Which management processes and procedures worked well?
- Which management processes and procedures caused problems?
- Was it simple to achieve the required quality?
- Which quality processes worked well?
- Are there any shortcomings to be found in the quality processes?
- Have the risk measures worked?
- Were there any risks that were not identified beforehand?
- Was the planned tolerance used?
- Was the training in management, quality, delivery processes and procedures adequate?
- Has the training produced visible advantages?
- Have the supporting tools proved their value?

With an ICT project the following subdivision is useful for the Lessons Report (D12):

- project management;
- requirements;
- change control;
- links between systems;
- realization;
- testing;
- data conversion;
- post implementation support;
- infrastructure and technolgy.

Based on the weak and strong points identified, the project team formulate lessons and recommendations for each topic.

8.27 Project Board Actions/Decisions (B27)

	Mandate (D1)	Project Brief (D3)	PID (D4)	Status Report (D6)	Highlights Report (D5)	End Project Report (D7)
Used in				✓		

Project Board actions/decisions <yy-mm-dd> <project		
#	Action/Decision	Steps taken	Results/subsequent steps

With this building block the project manager or project support officer (if available within the project) records the actions and decisions of the Project Board. They stipulate who is responsible for the result and when the actions have to be concluded. The project manager or project support officer disseminates the list with action points and decisions as soon as possible after the Project Board meeting. In the meantime they check the status of the actions, so that all of these can be followed up at the following Project Board meeting.

Discussions concerning content do not belong in the Project Board. If a point has not been addressed satisfactorily, it is resubmitted at the next Project Board meeting in an Exceptions Report (D8) or in the building block Decisions to be taken (B23) of the Status Report (D6).

8.28 Customer Satisfaction (B28)

	Mandate (D1)	Project Brief (D3)	PID (D4)	Status Report (D6)	Highlights Report (D5)	End Project Report (D7)
Used in						✓

Customer satisfaction of project manager's effort and results

Project:	How do you evaluate the:	Score (1-10)
Project Manager:	1. Extent to which the objective of the assignment has been achieved?	
	2. Approach/procedure used?	
Evaluation Period:	3. Effort of the project manager?	
	4.	
Completed by:	5.	
	6.	
Date:	Average score =	
Initials:		

Comments: (Think of points that can be improved, strong points and other comments)

The stakeholders each complete the Customer Satisfaction form. Their completed forms provide an insight into the functioning of the project. The combination of these forms completed for different projects provides a basis for reviewing these projects. In addition the Comments field creates the opportunity of becoming aware of the strengths of the project manager and the project team, together with the lessons learned. The executives of the project manager can translate these lessons learned into development agreements. The average rating of all project team and customer forms (refer also to the Project Team Satisfaction (B29) building block) of all projects and project managers provides a reliable indication of how the project management organisation is functioning.

8.29 Project Team Satisfaction (B29)

	Mandate (D1)	Project Brief (D3)	PID (D4)	Status Report (D6)	Highlights Report (D5)	End Project Report (D7)
Used in						✓

Project Team satisfaction of project manager's effort and results

Project:	How do you evaluate the:	Score (1-10)
Project Manager:	1. Project set-up and organisational structure?	
	2. Project planning and control?	
Evaluation Period:	3. Effort of the project manager?	
	4. Finances and management?	
Completed by:	5. Communication?	
Date:	Average score =	
Initials:		

Comments: (Think of points that can be improved, strong points and other comments)

The project team employees complete the Project Team Satisfaction form. Through this an insight is gained into how effectively the project manager has functioned. The combination of forms from different projects provides a basis for reviewing the respective project managers. In addition the Comments field provides the opportunity of identifying the strengths of the project manager and the lessons learned. The executives of the project manager can translate these lessons learned into development agreements.

The average of all Project Team and Customer Satisfaction forms (also refer to the Customer Satisfaction (B28) building block) of all projects and project managers provides a reliable impression of how the project management organisation is functioning.

In reverse the project manager – as the functioning executive – can give feedback to project employees. Conveying this information to the executive hierarchy from the project team member enables them to evaluate project team members on the basis of their effort in the project.

8.30 Issue Register (B30)

			project name:			
1 Objective: - keeping track of all project issues; - allocation of a unique number to a project issue.						
2 Short explanation of the project:						
3 Type: W = Request for change, F = Finding, I = Issue, Q = Question						
ID	Type	Recorded by	Date recorded	Date of last change	Description	Status
1	RfC					open
2	I					closed
3						review
						analysis

The issue register is a tool that enables the project manager to record all project issues in a structured manner. In this way the issues do not get lost. For each issue the type is described, as well as the request for change, the findings and any associated questions. The project manager determines the priority of the issues, so that the most important ones are addressed first. Open (outstanding) issues require action.

8.31 Risk Register (B31)

project name:										
1 Objective: to keep track of the status of all project risks										
2 Short explanation of the project:										
3 Type: B = Business/organisation, P = Project, S = Stage										
ID	Type	Risk description	Owner	Date recorded	Date of last change	Limit date	Possibility	Impact	Risk	Measures	Status
1											
2											
3											

The Risk Register shows the risks, the owner of these risks, the planning of the measures and their status. In addition it is wise to record in this log to what extent risks threaten the project. This prevents time being wasted on removing negligible risks. An accepted formula for this is: risk = possibility × impact

Possibility: 0 to 4 (impossible, low, average, high, certain).
Impact: 0 to 4 (imperceptible, low, fairly serious, very serious, catastrophic).
Risk: from uncomfortable (risk taken into account) to damaging (prevention is better than cure) to fatal (to be prevented at all costs).

Risk analysis is a procedure that provides insight into foreseeable problems in a project. To diminish the risks, precautionary actions and countermeasures are taken. The step-by-step plan below describes how it is done:

1. What can go wrong?
2. What problem can the risk cause in the project?
3. How big is the risk?
4. What possible causes can the problem have?
5. What is the likelihood of these causes?
6. What are possible preventative actions or countermeasures?
7. What are the alternatives or make-shift solutions?

This step-by-step plan is to be dealt with from the outside inwards and from the inside outwards. With the first approach, those involved look at the general risks that can occur within the organisation. Next they evaluate the project risks emanating from these. With the second procedure those involved begin with the project. Next they explore the environment. Design standard risk analysis questionnaires for your organisation and maintain them.

8.32 Lessons Learned Register (B32)

	project name:						
1 Objective: to summarise all lessons learned							
2 Short explanation of the project:							
ID	Product-name	Lesson learned	Submitted by	Responsible	Date recorded	Comment	
1							
2							
3							

The Lessons Learned Register is an aid for compiling the Lessons Report at the stage end or the completion of the project. During the project the project manager keeps the log up to date. This prevents lessons learned from getting lost and makes it possible to improve procedures in the projects. The following are possible topics for the report:

- reasons for changes in the planning;
- lessons learned regarding quality control and project management processes;
- lessons learned regarding methods and techniques;
- recommendations for improving the project management method;
- evaluation of the quality review results;
- procedures of the project team;
- procedures of the Project Board.

For every lesson learned, ask the following questions:

- what went well?
- what can be improved?
- what are the recommendations?

Ensure that the lessons learned are disseminated throughout the organisation. This will help to prevent mistakes from being made in subsequent projects. Also see to it that future projects benefit from the experience of those things that went well.

8.33 Action list (B33)

			project name:				
1 Objective: to keep track of the status of all actions. This summary does not replace the project planning.							
2 Short explanation of the project::							

ID	Product-name	Necessary action	Submitted by	Responsible	Status	Date recorded	Comment
1					Open		
2					Closed		
3					Waiting for		

The Action list is a tool for the project manager to keep all current actions up to date. The Action list is not a replacement for the project planning. A daily updated Action list makes it possible to hand over current actions in a structured manner in the event of serious problems (for example the sudden absence of the project manager). The Action list furthermore makes it possible for the project manager to keep pace with important events and information in respect of every action. The Action list is concerned with information that is not indicated in other building blocks.

List of Terms PRINCE2 (ed. 2005)

Term	Description
Acceptance Criteria	A prioritised list of criteria that the final product(s) must meet before the customer will accept them; a measurable definition of what must be done for the final product to be acceptable to the customer. They should be defined as part of the Project Brief and agreed between customer and supplier no later than the project initiation stage. They should be documented in the Project Initiation Document.
Acceptance of the completion of support and management	Formal acceptance from those who are to support and manage the product. The method of acceptance can vary from a simple letter of acceptance to a detailed maintenance contract.
Activity network	A flow diagram showing the activities of a plan and their interdependencies. The network shows each activity's duration, earliest start and finish times, latest start and finish times and float. Also known as 'planning network'.
Baseline	A snapshot; a position or situation that is recorded. Although the position may be updated later, the baseline remains unchanged and available as a reminder of the original state and as a comparison against the current position. Products that have passed their quality checks and are approved are baselined products. Anything 'baselined' should be under version control in configuration management and 'frozen', i.e. no changes to that version are allowed.
Benefits	The positive outcomes, quantified or unquantified, that a project is being undertaken to deliver and that justify the investment.
Business Case	Information that describes the justification for setting up and continuing a PRINCE2 project. It provides the reasons (and answers the question: 'Why?') for the project. An outline Business Case should be in the Project Mandate. Its existence is checked as part of the Project Brief, and a revised, fuller version appears in the Project Initiation Document. It is updated at key points, such as end stage assessments, throughout the project.
Change authority	A group to which the Project Board may delegate responsibility for the consideration of Requests for Change. The change authority is given a budget and can approve changes within that budget.
Change budget	The money allocated to the change authority to be spent on authorised Requests for Change.
Change control	The procedure to ensure that the processing of all Project Issues is controlled, including submission, analysis and decision making.
Communication Plan	Part of the Project Initiation Document describing how the project's stakeholders and interested parties will be kept informed during the project.
Concession	An Off-Specification that is accepted by the Project Board without corrective action.

Configuration	All the products of which realisation and/or control are to be managed. In the context of a project, the configuration of the project result is the total of the deliverables.
Configuration audit	A comparison of the latest version number and status of all products shown in the configuration library records against the information held by the product authors.
Configuration control	Configuration control is concerned with physically controlling receipt and issue of products, keeping track of product status, protecting finished products and controlling any changes to them.
Configuration Item	A product of which realisation and/or control must be managed.
Configuration Item Records	The registration of all important information for realising and managing a configuration item.
Configuration Librarian	The person responsible for configuration management within a project. The Configuration Librarian reports to the Project Manager.
Configuration management	A discipline, normally supported by software tools, that gives management precise control over its assets (for example, the products of a project), covering planning, identification, control, status accounting and verification of the products.
Configuration Management Plan	The plans describing how deliverables in a project are managed in a clear and structured manner.
Contingency budget	The amount of money required to implement a contingency plan. If the Project Board approves a contingency plan, it would normally set aside a contingency budget, which would only be called upon if the contingency plan had to be implemented when the associated risk occurs. See also Contingency plan.
Contingency plan	A plan that provides details of the measures to be taken if a defined risk should occur. The plan is only implemented if the risk occurs. A contingency plan is prepared where other actions (risk prevention, reduction or transfer) are not possible, too expensive or the current view is that the cost of the risk occurring does not sufficiently outweigh the cost of taking avoiding action - but the risk cannot be simply accepted. The Project Board can see that, should the risk occur, there is a plan of action to counter it. If the Project Board agrees that this is the best form of action, it would put aside a contingency budget, the cost of the contingency plan, only to be used if the risk occurs.
Critical path	This is the line connecting the start of an activity network with the final activity in that network through those activities with zero float, i.e. those activities where any delay will delay the time of the entire end date of the plan. There may be more than one such path. The sum of the activity durations on the critical path will determine the end date of the plan.
Customer	The person or group who commissioned the work and will benefit from the end results.
Customer's Quality Expectations	A statement from the customer about the quality expected from the final product. This should be obtained during the start-up of a project in Preparing a Project Brief (SU4) as an important feed into Planning Quality (IP1), where it is matched against the Project Approach and the standards that will need to be applied in order to achieve that quality.

Daily Log	A record of jobs to do or to check that others have done, commitments from the author or others, important events, decisions or discussions. A Daily Log should be kept by the Project Manager and any Team Managers.
Demand	A description of a required characteristic of a product or service to be delivered.
Earned value analysis	Earned value analysis is a method for measuring project performance. It indicates how much of the work done so far and the task, assignment or resources.
End Project Report	A report given by the Project Manager to the Project Board that confirms the handover of all products and provides an updated Business Case and an assessment of how well the project has done against its Project Initiation Document.
End result	The product or service in a project for delivery.
End stage assessment	The review by the Project Board and Project Manager of the End Stage Report to decide whether to approve the next Stage Plan (unless the last stage has now been completed). According to the size and criticality of the project, the review may be formal or informal. The approval to proceed should be documented as an important management product.
End Stage Report	A report given by the Project Manager to the Project Board at the end of each management stage of the project. This provides information about the project performance during the stage and the project status at stage end.
Exception	A situation where it can be forecast that there will be a deviation beyond the tolerance levels agreed between the Project Manager and the Project Board (or between the Project Board and corporate or programme management, or between a Team Manager and the Project Manager).
Exception assessment	This is a meeting of the Project Board to approve (or reject) an Exception Plan.
Exception Plan	This is a plan that often follows an Exception Report. For a Team Plan exception, it covers the period from the present to the end of the Work Package; for a Stage Plan exception, it covers the period from the present to the end of the current stage. If the exception were at a project level, the Project Plan would be replaced.
Exception Report	Description of the exception situation, its impact, options, recommendation and impact of the recommendation to the Project Board. This report is prepared by the relevant manager to inform the next higher level of management of the situation.
Executive	The single individual with overall responsibility for ensuring that a project meets its objectives and delivers the projected benefits. This individual should ensure that the project or programme maintains its business focus, that it has clear authority and that the work, including risks, is actively managed. The Executive is the chairperson of the Project Board, representing the customer, and is the owner of the Business Case.

Feasibility study	A feasibility study is an early study of a problem to assess if a solution is feasible. The study will normally scope the problem, identify and explore a number of solutions, and make a recommendation on what action to take. Part of the work in developing options is to calculate an outline Business Case for each as one aspect of comparison.
Follow-on Action Recommendation	A report that can be used as input to the process of creating a Business Case/Project Mandate for any follow-on PRINCE2 project and for recording any followon instructions covering incomplete products or outstanding Project Issues.
Gantt chart	This is a diagram of a plan's activities against a time background, showing start and end times and resources required.
Highlight Report	Time-driven report from the Project Manager to the Project Board on stage progress.
Issue Log	Contains all Project Issues including Requests for Change raised during the project. Project Issues are each allocated a unique number and are filed in the Issue Log under the appropriate status. See also Project Issue.
Lessons Learned Log	An informal collection of good and bad lessons learned about the management and specialist processes and products as the project progresses. At the end of the project, it is formalised and structured into a Lessons Learned Report. See also Lessons Learned Report.
Lessons Learned Report	A report that describes the lessons learned in undertaking the project and includes statistics from the quality control of the project's management products. It is approved by the Project Board and then held centrally for the benefit of future projects.
Management product	A deliverable to be completed during the project in order to control the realisation of the deliverable and to ensure the quality to be delivered.
Notification of Project Closure	Advice from the Project Board to all stakeholders that the project is being closed and that the team members and supporting facilities such as space, material and access are no longer necessary from a certain date.
Notification of Project End	Notification from the Project Manager to the parties concerned that the project is nearly complete and also the signal to start the process Closing a Project.
Notification of Project Start	A report from the Project Board to the organisation where the project is being carried out to the effect that the project is being started and requesting the necessary supporting services be made available.
Notification of Stage End	Notification from the Project Manager to the parties concerned that the Stage is nearly complete and at the same time the signal for starting the process Managing Stage Boundaries.
Off-Specification	Something that should be provided by the project, but currently is not (or is forecast not to be) provided. This might be a missing product or a product not meeting its specifications. It is one type of Project Issue.
Post-implementation review	See: Post-project review.

Post-project review	One or more reviews held after project closure to determine if the expected benefits have been obtained. Also known as post-implementation review.
Post-Project Review Plan	The document laying down how, when and by whom the current benefits and those to be realised will be measured and recorded in order to establish whether the Business Case of the project will be realised.
PRINCE2	A method that supports some selected aspects of project management. The acronym stands for PRojects IN Controlled Environments.
PRINCE2 project	A project whose product(s) can be defined at its start sufficiently precisely so as to be measurable against predefined metrics and that is managed according to the PRINCE2 method.
Process	That which must be done to bring about a particular result in terms of information to be gathered, decisions to be made and results to be achieved.
Producer	This role represents the creator(s) of a product that is the subject of a quality review. Typically, it will be filled by the person who has produced the product or who has led the team responsible.
Product	Any input to or output from a project. PRINCE2 distinguishes between management products (which are produced as part of the management or quality processes of the project) and specialist products (which are those products that make up the final deliverable). A product may itself be a collection of other products.
Product Breakdown Structure	A hierarchy of all the products to be produced during a plan.
Product Checklist	A list of the major products of a plan, plus key dates in their delivery.
Product Description	A description of a product's purpose, composition, derivation and quality criteria. It is produced at planning time, as soon as possible after the need for the product is identified.
Product Flow Diagram	A diagram showing the sequence of production and interdependencies of the products listed in a Product Breakdown Structure.
Product life span	The product's total life span from the original idea to make the product up to and including replacement or dismantling of the product. Several projects may be carried out during the product life span such as a feasibility study, realisation, an upgrade or renovation and the final replacement or dismantling.
Product Status Account	A report on the status of the product. This includes, among other things, information on the current status, the previous status and the changes planned and implemented.
Product-based planning	A four-step technique leading to a comprehensive plan based on creation and delivery of required outputs. The technique considers prerequisite products, quality requirements and the dependencies between products.
Programme	A portfolio of projects selected, planned and managed in a co-ordinated way.
Progress report	A report on the progress of a Work Package submitted by the Team Manager to the Project Manager at set times or intervals.
Progress review	An assessment of the progress of the project at team level at set times or intervals.

Project	A temporary organisation that is created for the purpose of delivering one or more business products according to a specified Business Case.
Project Approach	A description of the way in which the work of the project is to be approached. For example: Are we building a product from scratch or buying in a product that already exists? Are the technology and products that we can use constrained by decisions taken at programme level?
Project Assurance	The Project Board's responsibilities to assure itself that the project is being conducted correctly.
Project Brief	A description of what the project is to do; a refined and extended version of the Project Mandate, which the Project Board approves and which is input to project initiation.
Project Initiation Document (PID)	A logical document that brings together the key information needed to start the project on a sound basis and to convey that information to all concerned with the project.
Project Issue	A term used to cover any concern, query, Request for Change, suggestion or Off-Specification raised during the project. They can be about anything to do with the project.
Project life cycle	The total life cycle of a project from start to finish. A project starts following authorisation of carrying out of the initial stage by the Project Board and finishes with confirmation of project closure by the Project Board.
Project management	Management tasks required in order to realise the project outcome. This includes planning, organising, monitoring and control of all aspects of the project and the motivation of all persons involved.
Project Management Structure	The total management structure required in order to initiate, set up and manage a project. The Project Management Structure includes corporate or programme management, the Project Board, the Project Manager, the Team Managers plus the supporting and assurance roles of Project Support and Project Assurance.
Project management team	Covers the entire management structure of Project Board, Project Manager, plus any Team Manager, Project Assurance and Project Support roles.
Project Manager	The person given the authority and responsibility to manage the project on a day-to-day basis to deliver the required products within the constraints agreed with the Project Board.
Project Mandate	Information created externally to the project that forms the terms of reference and is used to start up the PRINCE2 project.
Project organisation	Temporary organisation responsible for setting up, carrying out and managing a project. Project organisation includes the Project Board, the Project Manager, the Team Managers, Project Support, Project Assurance and project staff.
Project owner	Is not a PRINCE2 term but is used in many organisations and is equivalent to "Executive".

Project Plan	A high-level plan showing the major products of the project, when they will be delivered and at what cost. An initial Project Plan is presented as part of the Project Initiation Document. This is revised as information on actual progress appears. It is a major control document for the Project Board to measure actual progress against expectations.
Project Quality Plan	A plan defining the key quality criteria, quality control and audit processes to be applied to project management and specialist work in the PRINCE2 project. It will be part of the text in the Project Initiation Document.
Project Support	An administrative role in the project management team. Project Support can be in the form of advice and help with project management tools, guidance, administrative services such as filing, and the collection of actual data. The provision of any Project Support on a formal basis is optional. Tasks either need to be done by the Project Manager or delegated to a separate body and this will be driven by the needs of the individual project and Project Manager.
Project Support Office	A unit set up to provide certain administrative services for one or more projects. The Project Support Office often provides its services for several projects.
Quality	The totality of features and characteristics of a product or service that bear on its ability to satisfy stated and implied needs.
Quality Log	Contains all planned and completed quality activities. The Quality Log is used by the Project Manager and Project Assurance as part of reviewing progress.
Quality review	A quality review is a quality checking technique with a specific structure, defined roles and procedure designed to ensure a product's completeness and adherence to standards. The participants are drawn from those with an interest in the product and those with the necessary skills to review its correctness.
Quality system	The complete set of quality standards, procedures and responsibilities for a site or organisation.
Recommendation for Project Closure	A recommendation prepared by the Project Manager for the Project Board (at the end of the project) for sending a recommendation for project closure to all stakeholders as soon as the Project Board agrees that the Project can be closed.
Request for Change	A request for adapting the current specification of the required product. A change request is a Project Issue.
Reviewer	A person asked to review a product that is the subject of a quality review.
Risk	Risk can be defined as uncertainty of outcome, whether positive opportunity or negative threat. Every project has risks associated with it. Project management has the task of identifying risks that apply and taking appropriate steps to take advantage of opportunities that may arise and avoid, reduce or react to threats.
Risk deadline	The deadline on which and the period in which a risk occurs.
Risk Log	Contains all information about the risks, their analysis, countermeasures and status. Also known as Risk Register.
Risk profile	A graphical representation of information normally found in the Risk Log.

Risk tolerance line	The risk tolerance line is one drawn between risks that can be accepted or for which suitable actions have been planned, and risks that that are considered sufficiently serious to require referral to the next higher level of project authority.
Senior Supplier	The Project Board role that provides knowledge and experience of the main discipline(s) involved in the production of the project's deliverable(s). Represents the supplier interests within the project and provides supplier resources.
Senior User	The Project Board role accountable for ensuring that user needs are specified correctly and that the solution meets those needs.
Specialist product	A product that has to be made during the project as part of the specifications. It may be part of the final outcome or a semi-finished product on which one or more subsequent product depends.
Specification	A detailed statement of what the user wants in terms of products, what these should look like, what they should do and with what they should interface.
Sponsor	Not a specific PRINCE2 role but often used to mean the major driving force of a project. May be the equivalent of Executive or corporate/programme management.
Stage	A stage is the section of the project that the Project Manager is managing on behalf of the Project Board at any one time, at the end of which the Project Board wishes to review progress to date, the state of the Project Plan, Business Case and risks, and the next Stage Plan in order to decide whether to continue with the project.
Stage Plan	A detailed plan for the Project Manager for management control during the management stage of a project. For the Project Board, the Stage Plan is also the basis for authorising the start of the respective stage and making the necessary staff and resources available.
Stakeholders	Parties with an interest in the execution and outcome of a project. They would include business streams affected by or dependent on the outcome.
Supplier	The group or groups responsible for the supply of the project's specialist products.
Team Manager	A role that may be employed by the Project Manager or Senior Supplier to manage the work of project team members.
Tolerance	The permissible deviation above and below a plan's estimate of time and cost without escalating the deviation to the next level of management. Separate tolerance figures should be given for time and cost. There may also be tolerance levels for quality, scope, benefit and risk. Tolerance is applied at project, stage and team levels.
User(s)	The person or group who will use the final deliverable(s) of the project.
Work Package	The set of information relevant to the creation of one or more products. It will contain a description of the work, the Product Description(s), details of any constraints on production such as time and cost, interfaces, and confirmation of the agreement between the Project Manager and the person or Team Manager who is to implement the Work Package that the work can be done within the constraints.

Bibliography

Atos Consulting Trends Institute, *Benchmark ICT Projectmanagement Nederland 2006, Progressie in professie?*, 2006.

Atos Consulting Trends Institute, *Benchmark Projectmanagement Nederland 2007, Transformatie middels Project Portfolio Management*, 2007.

Atos Consulting Trends Institute, *Benchmark Projectmanagement 2008, Transparantie tussen Project en Organisatie*, 2008.

Atkinson, C., Beyond Bullet Points, *Using PowerPoint to create presentations that inform, motivate, and inspire*, Microsoft Press, 2005.

Belbin, R., *Management Teams, Why They Succeed or Fail*, 2nd edition, 2008.

Bos, J., E. Haiting, *Projectmatig Creëren 2.0*, Scriptum, Schiedam, 2006.

Dunnink, H.W., R.N.A.M. Laane , H.C. ten Zweege, *Trends in Project Performance Improvement*, Capgemini Nederland B.V., Utrecht, 2005.

Gevers, T., W. Hendrickx, *Kansrijk Risicomanagement in projecten, practische leidraad voor het managen van risico's en kansen in projecten*, Academic Service, 2001.

Groote, G.P., Sasse C.J., Slikker, P., *Projecten leiden, methoden en technieken voor projectmatig werken*, Het Spectrum, Utrecht, 2005.

Hedeman, B.H., *De nieuwe PRINCE-heerlijk, Methode voor het leiden van succesvolle projecten*, 2de druk Academic Service 2005.

Hedeman, B.H., Frediksz, H., G. Vis van Heemst, *Projectmanagement based on PRINCE2*, Van Haren Publishing, 2004.

Hill, G.M., *The Complete Project Management Office Handbook*, ESI International, 2004.

Janssen, P., *PRINCE2 Compact*, Pearson Education Benelux BV, 2007.

Janssen, P., *Projectmanagement volgens PRINCE2*, Pearson Education Benelux BV, 2005.

Kendall, G.I., Rollins, S.C., PMP, *Advanced Project Portfolio Management and the PMO. Multiplying ROI at warp speed*, J. Ross Publishing, 2003.

Kerzner, H., *Project Management, A systems approach to planning, scheduling and controlling*, John Wiley & sons, 2003.

Light, M., Stang, D.B., *Magic Quadrant for IT Project and Portfolio Management, 2007*, Gartner RAS Core Research Note G00149082, 2007.

Molen, M. van der, *PRINCE2 voor opdrachtgevers*, 3de druk Van Haren Publishing, 2006.

Mulder, N., F. Wijnstra, *De kleine prinses*, Uitgeverij Dialoog, 2008.

OGC, *Managing Successful Projects with PRINCE2: The PRINCE2 Manual*, Office of Government Commerce, 2009.

OGC, *People Issues and PRINCE2*, Office of Government Commerce, 2001.

OGC, *Business Benefits Through Project Management*, Office of Government Commerce, 2002.

Onna, M. van, A. Koning, *De kleine PRINCE2*, 5de druk, Academic Service, 2007.

Portman, H.P., *Het Storyboard en de highlight rapportage*, ProjectManager, December 2005, p. 20-21. Also released at www.serendipi-tijd.nl.

Portny, S. E., *Project Management for Dummies*, Hungry Minds, 2001.

Riso, D. R., R. Hudson, *Enneagram basisboek, De negen persoonlijkheidstypen in kaart gebracht*, Becht, 2005

Saint-Exupéry, A. de, *The Little Prince*. Wordsworth Children's Classics, N.Y.

Tucker, C., Gartner, March 2006 Premier Report, *Taking your PMO to the next stage*, 2006.

Visser, C., G.L. Schlundt Bodien, *Doen wat werkt, oplossingsgericht werken in organisaties*, Kluwer 2005.

About the author

Henny Portman studied Electronics (HTS, Utrecht) and Business Administration (Open University). Among other things he worked at Tiel Utrecht Verzekeringen for 15 years as head of Systems Development. During this period he was a member of the Dutch COBOL committee and the AMBI T2 examinations committee. He also served as chairman of the PDI programming languages stream. After a consultancy assignment at ING Fatum in Paramaribo, he worked for five years as head of IT Management Netherlands at ING Investment Management Nederland.

Subsequently he was head of the Project Management Office at ING Investment Management Europe. In this position he controlled the entire project portfolio and provided guidance to business project and programme managers. He was responsible for standards, methods and techniques, coaching and taking care of training courses.

As Regional PMO Head he is currently accountable for the entire projects portfolio of ING Insurance Central Europe and is responsible for setting up and directing the PMOs in Poland, Russia, Hungary, the Czech Republic, Slovakia, Romania, Bulgaria, Spain and Greece.

Henny Portman is a member of the international project group, the Project Management Centre of Excellence (PM CoE) of the ING Group and is responsible for the Project Management Certification working group.

He is co-owner and initiator of the PM Education Indicator, www.serendipi-tijd.nl, a knowledge portal for project and change managers as well as executives.

From the pen of Henny Portman several articles on the topic of project management have appeared in print.

Index

A
Acceptance Criteria 14, 25, 46
actions and decisions 102
Antoine de Saint-Exupéry 1
Architecture 14, 91
architecture and information security.... 92
archiving 51

B
Belbin 40, 86
Budget 15
Budget details................... 25, 28
building block concepts 12, 62
building blocks................ VI, 6, 13
Business Case................ 4, 6, 7, 14
Business Process Aspects............... 26

C
Change Procedure 33
Closing a Project 3, 4
Communication plan............. 26, 94
Controlling a Stage................. 4
Cost Benefit Cash Flow 72
Customer Satisfaction............. 61, 103

D
Decisions to be taken 29, 98
Directing a Project 4
Document management............... 55

E
Earned Value Analysis 29, 56, 89
End Project Report............ 30, 32, 43
executive 13, 20

F
Follow-on Action Recommendations 30

G
Gartner 55

H
Highlights Report 15, 29, 31

I
Information Security 14, 26
Initiating a Project 3
Internal costs 25, 42, 88
Internal Rate of Return (IRR) ... 22, 42, 74
Issue Register 7, 33, 105

K
Key Process Indicator (KPI) 40

L
lessons learned 7, 32
Lessons Report................. 7, 32, 35

M
Managing Product Delivery 4
Managing Stage Boundaries 4
Mandate....................... 6, 20

N
Net Present Value (NPV) 22, 42, 74

O
Organisation 4
out-of-pocket...................... 43

P
Payback Period................ 22, 73, 74
PID 14
Planning...................... 4, 15, 41
processes........................... 3
Process Model 2, 3
Product Breakdown 23, 49
project and portfolio management
    systems.................... 55, 58
project approach................. 23, 75
Project Background 21, 70

Project Board 4, 9
Project Brief 7, 14, 23
Project Initiation Document (PID) . . . 7, 25
Project Management Office (PMO) 46
project organisation 5, 38
project owner 57

Q
Quality 5
Quality Check 50
Quality Plan 14, 26, 46
quality requirements 23, 26, 46

R
Recapitulation 30
Resources 15
Risk Register 7, 84, 106
Risks 14, 21, 34, 72

S
Scope 1, 20, 21
Senior Supplier 25, 40, 86
Senior User 25, 40, 86
SMART' templates 57
stakeholders 11, 19, 23
Starting up a Project 3
storyboard 13
Storyboarding 12, 16
story-lines 46, 57

T
Templates 11, 16, 50

V
Value Chain 23, 77

W
work package 7, 23, 27